Outsourcing to India – A Legal Handbook

Bharat Vagadia

Outsourcing to India – A Legal Handbook

With 10 Figures

Springer

Bharat Vagadia
53 Brampton Grove
London HA3 8LE
United Kingdom
bharat.vagadia@op2i.com
www.op2i.com

ISBN 978-3-642-09136-0 e-ISBN 978-3-540-72220-5

Springer is a part of Springer Science+Business Media

springer.com

Cover-design: WMX Design GmbH, Heidelberg

I would like to dedicate the book to my late father
Khimji Karsan Vagadia

Foreword

When Bharat first asked me to provide a foreword for this book I was flattered and somewhat surprised. I'm not at lawyer and cannot hope to understand the intricate legal complexities of India and outsourcing, yet I can recall doing my own research into the topic back in 2003 when I was writing my own book for Springer, 'Outsourcing to India: The Offshore Advantage'. That book was published in 2004 and was so popular that I managed to overhaul it with extra chapters for a second edition just a year later in 2005.

'Outsourcing to India: The Offshore Advantage' featured just a single chapter on law, as part of an overview on the whole Indian outsourcing experience. Bharat has now taken my humble offering of a single chapter many steps further by producing his own comprehensive volume on how the law is an important factor to take into account in any outsourcing relationship.

In many areas of the outsourcing relationship, it is the skill of the legal counsel that can make or break a deal. Fears over the enforceability of contracts, or the protection of sensitive data, or intellectual property disputes are all examples of key areas where the business management rely on the legal team to not only understand the law itself, but to understand how smooth contractual relationships can help the business and their customers.

In producing this volume, Bharat has done the entire world outsourcing community a favour – not just the legal community alone. This book deserves to be widely distributed and read by anyone managing outsourcing contracts that involve companies in India. I hope it will encourage a wider understanding of how to work with EU and Indian law to create a better outsourcing relationship, for the end user and the supplier.

London, June 2007

Mark Kobayashi-Hillary
DirectorUK National Outsourcing Association
www.markhillary.com

Preface

This book differs from many others that have been published in the sphere of outsourcing, primarily because the aim of this book is not about the size of the outsourcing market, or the benefits or not of outsourcing: issues which have been discussed quite adequately by many other books. The book briefly introduces and skims over such matters. It does not attempt to forecast the market or indeed preach the benefits, but merely summarises the various forecasts that many experts in the field have produced – the aim of which is to create a context within which the book has been written.

Outsourcing to India – a legal handbook attempts to outline the critical legal factors that an enterprise needs to consider when contemplating outsourcing services to companies based in India – these concerns need to be encapsulated within a legal contract - it examines the risks that commonly arise in outsourcing contracts and suggests ways in which these risks can be allocated.

The book provides a framework to ensure that having made the decision to outsource, appropriate resource and legal conditions are considered and addressed to ensure the relationship that a company is about to embark on, will result in the best possible outcome for the company, and in the event that the relationship doesn't work, the company can walk away without having to pay a ransom or face other contractual strangle-holds.

The book is written for all the stakeholders involved in the process of outsourcing, which include:

- Company Strategists who need to decide if outsourcing is right for their business.
- Business Managers who need to ensure that outsourcing can be appropriately integrated within the organisation.
- Process Managers who will need to develop quantified objectives for the outsourcing deal and define the operating and service level agreements.
- IT Managers who will need to ensure that the infrastructure and IT systems are adequate and fully integrated into the outsourcing service provider.
- Procurement Managers who will be negotiating the deal.
- Senior Managers who will need to understand the risks-reward trade off.

- In house and external lawyers and legal council who will be trying to minimise any un-necassary exposure to risk.
- Consultants advising firms on outsourcing.
- Service providers, servicing the outsourcing needs of customers - who need to understand how they can assist their clients and prospective clients get the most from outsourcing at the lowest risk possible.

In addition the book will serve as reference material for those studying and teaching Commercial law, International law, Data protection and Intellectual Property Rights at universities and colleges.

Although the book concentrates on India as an outsourcing destination, the principles, concepts and risk minimisation tactics are equally applicable to outsourcing to any other destination.

This book is not a substitute to specific legal and commercial advice that specialists legal advisors and consultants can bring to the outsourcing process. This book however, should serve as a guide to ensure the customer is fully aware of the issues, risks and possible risk mitigation strategies that can be employed.

It will also ensure all the personnel involved in the outsourcing process understand the full gambit of issues that need to be addressed. It also serves as a useful reminder that in some cases only good planning from the start, not the insertion of legal clauses into the contract, will mitigate risk throughout the lifecycle of the agreement.

I would like to thank everyone involved in the production of this book. My editors at Springer in Germany; Brigitte Reschke and Manuela Ebert have given me the inspiration for completing the book and in the process have given me a pretty useful lesson on how to use MS Word.

I would also like to thank Peter Breakey, a senior lecturer at Northumbria University who assisted me in developing the thoughts for writing the book.

Jenny Nolan, who assisted in proof reading the book – a pretty hefty task for someone without a legal or outsourcing background, and Steve Hodson and Mark Morris who provided me with some useful issues of relevance in the area of SLAs.

Finally I would like to thank my family and in particular my wife Bhavna, who has supported me and put up with my absence whilst I sat in the study writing the book, whilst she looked after our daughter, Divyamayi, who decided to arrive early in this world and threw my original plan somewhat array.

If I have omitted anyone, it is not that I am un-grateful, but merely that I must be getting old and becoming forgetful - please do accept my apologies.

If I have made any errors, omissions or misjudgements then it is entirely my fault. Please do contact me if you have any comments, corrections, suggestions or seek further advice.

Bharat K Vagadia
London, June 2007

www.op2i.com

Table of contents

1. Background and snapshot of key issues

1.1 Context

A recent survey by Nelson Hall[1] and the National Outsourcing Association off one hundred sourcing managers at end-users companies, found that the leading criteria in the selection of a suitable offshore location was the availability of legal protection - factors such as infrastructure, political stability and others came lower in the list.

From the list of outsourcing / offshoring countries that have emerged and which are likely to remain the most significant, India is the leading contender for the top spot.

1.2 Background

Outsourcing is nothing new. From the 1600's and earlier, the British have had work done for them abroad, even if it was simply the processing of sugar in Antigua.

Outsourcing is essentially an elaborate description for an arrangement whereby a company carves out certain services that it has been providing internally and retains a third party to provide these services. Offshoring is sometimes described as outsourcing to service providers in other countries.

Many authors use such descriptions interchangeably, and in the context of outsourcing to India, both descriptions can be deemed appropriate. However the preference within this book is to use outsourcing as a general description, as offshoring tends to imply that a company simply moves its operations overseas – something which is quite separate to contracting with another entity overseas.

In its basic form, outsourcing is a form of risk management. In going down the outsourcing route, companies conclude that the risk of having another firm perform and manage a business process is less than doing it internally. Companies

---

1 A BPO analyst firm.

may decide that the trade-off between the risks and reward of outsourcing to an international provider outweighs that of outsourcing to a domestic provider.

There are two approaches to specifying an outsourcing contract, on the one hand you can specify the contract in terms of output e.g. number of calls answered by a call centre, or on the other hand you can specify an activity to cover a service level e.g. the provision of a call centre that answers calls within a set period, e.g. 10 seconds for instance. Basic services tend to be based on the former, being very much transactional[2], whereas the latter are more strategic in nature and tend to be based on a partnership approach, where the outsourcing provider provides a service to meet customer needs in any manner not be strictly tied to type of activity or payment.

These two forms can essentially be categorised as either Information Technology Outsourcing (ITO)[3] or Business Process Outsourcing (BPO).

Information Technology Outsourcing (ITO) and Business Process Outsourcing (BPO) share many common features, but they are fundamentally different exercises:

- In an ITO (i.e. desktop management, network management, server management, application development), the customer's primary goal tends to be cost savings. The service provider generally tends to offer a commoditised[4] solution across a large set of customers with the same or similar needs.
- In a BPO (i.e. HR administration, finance & accounting, market research and analysis), the customer may seek cost savings, but typically it also targets other value added objectives. The solution offered to the customer tends to be far more tailored to the customer's particular needs.

Because BPO often targets these broader and deeper objectives, the contract process is lengthier and it is therefore much more important to ensure the contract is appropriate.

As is the case with respect to any material agreement, the structure of the outsourcing agreement is crucial because it embodies the rights, remedies, duties and obligations of the parties and provides a blueprint for the parties' relationship. These considerations are magnified in an outsourcing arrangement because:

---

2 A lower order effect upon a business, where the tasks tend to be non-core activities and where the service provided is very much standardised.

3 Information Technology is the automation of critical business functions insofar as those functions involve processing and storage of information.

4 A commoditised solution is generally a solution which is homogenous and can be sold to a range of customers. The solution in a sense becomes a commodity and can be sold without the need for any modification.

- The functions to be performed are typically business critical or strategically important; and
- The relationship between the service provider and the customer is typically of a longer duration and greater intimacy than the relationship created in other commercial contexts.

In many respects the outsourcing relationship is similar to a marriage – the primary goal is to have an understanding partner and to have a win-win relationship – quite independent of legal obligations and contracts. The main purpose of contracts is to regulate the relationship when things don't work out as anticipated. A good contract can serve as a deterrent against going to court. The actual process of jointly creating and discussing a contract can be a highly valuable process allowing the parties to develop a common understanding of the outsourcing relationship.

Outsourcing projects contrary to popular belief, typically do not take their disputes to court, because the outcome is uncertain and the possibility of damage to the reputation of both the outsourcing provider and the client is so great. For most firms, the contract is the first thing they prepare and the thing they argue over the longest, and the last thing they use.

1.2.1 Organisations outsource for a number of reasons

Traditionally, IT outsourcing in Europe, and particularly in the UK, was driven largely by the public sector. In recent years however, outsourcing from the public sector has slowed and the private sector has begun to grow. Now the public sector is once again growing and having a major impact upon the market.

Clearly the objectives set by outsourcing will differ and will be driven by internal processes, external market influences and in many cases will differ between those from the private sector and those from the public sector. Making a broad generalisation, those from the public sector tend to be much more cost focused, whilst those from the private sector have a number of different objectives, of which cost savings may be one.

Typical objectives desired from outsourcing include (particularly in the case of the private sector):

- Improving strategic positioning through increased focus on core functions.
- Improving competitiveness through operational performance improvements and access to cheaper and more specialist skills.
- Increasing control through process improvement.
- Reducction in costs through new technology or innovative practices.

The economics of offshore outsourcing provides a compelling reason for companies to outsource their business processes to companies in developing countries where labour costs are lower.

Service providers achieve savings from within their organisation that they can pass on to the outsourcing customer. These savings are achieved through economies of scale, as the outsourcer will be sharing the cost of its overheads over a number of customer clients from improved efficiency and skills of its staff and through its buying power, bringing down the costs of hardware, maintenance and consumables.

A report by Intellect UK[5], suggests that outsourcing does work for the majority of customers. Head count reduction, cost accountability and balance sheet advantages can exceed expectations. However, expectations about access to supplier skills and the potential for innovation are frequently exaggerated. The report suggests the chances of success can be increased with proper preparation and early involvement by those who will receive the service; the end users – typically the contract is arranged by the service provider and the customer's buyer or contract manager, without end user involvement.

Examples of recent successful outsourcing relationships include:

- The Virgin group outsourced business functions to India and South Africa, cutting its IT budget by 15%. Virgin's group chief information officer identified cost as the fundamental driver, although he stated there are specific skills that may come later[6].
- Norwich Union, the insurance company outsourced 500 IT jobs in an effort to build greater flexibility into its IT base, to better deal with peaks and troughs in demand. More than two thirds of the outsourced jobs went to Norwich Union's existing Indian IT outsourcing suppliers, Tata Consultancy Services and Wipro[7]. The company had 2,300 IT staff in-house and 2,000 staff outsourced. The company is increasingly outsourcing functions up the value chain, whereas traditionally they outsourced low-key application development roles, they are moving towards systems architecture, design strategy and more IT management roles[8].
- The UK Financial Services Authority (FSA) was also planning to outsource its core IT services including data centre, network, helpdesk, testing and desktop management in a five year deal with a single supplier to be announced sometime in 2007. Separately to its outsourcing deal, the FSA is also expected to out-

---

5 Expectations versus reality in outsourcing, Intellect UK.

6 Computer Weekly, 16th June 2005.

7 Tata Consultancy Services Ltd is a leading information technology consulting, services, and business process outsourcing organization. Wirpo is also a leading Indian BPO and IT outsourcing provider.

8 Computer Weekly, 19th September 2006.

source large parts of its application development function using a framework agreement[9].

- Recently the supermarket chain, Somerfield, signed a seven year deal with Tata Consultancy Services to outsource the management of its entire IT infrastructure to India – the deal is expected to cut its IT costs by a third over the life of the £33million deal. As part of the deal 115 or the 141 IT jobs at the customer's head quarters will be cut, but a 25 strong team was to be retained to manage the contract.

However outsourcing is not for everyone. Not long before the Somerfield deal, Supermarket chain Sainsbury pulled out of a 10 year, £1.7 billion IT outsourcing contract with Accenture[10].

Companies should evaluate their outsourcing decisions using a structured framework, which allows them to evaluate opportunities according to their risk exposure and the company's ability to manage and mitigate such risk. Companies should seek a comfort zone in which they are confident in their ability to manage the risk.

1.2.2 Outsourcing trends

There are a number of research reports which forecast the outsourcing market. Some of the more widely cited reports are listed below: although such reports tend to get outdated within a few months. New reports get published inevitably showing an even higher forecast for the outsourcing market. However analysing the trend is useful, as it demonstrates confidence in the outsourcing model:

- In Europe according to Gartner, there was a 40% increase in offshore outsourcing during 2003. Gartner expected the rest of Europe to catch up quickly and predicted that 75% of the medium to large size companies across Europe were considering offshoring services by 2005. The UK represented more than 35% of outsourcing business in Europe.
- Around the world, offshore outsourcing will continue to grow at a rate of more than 20% annually, according to Meta Group, becoming a $10 billion market within two years.
- Gartner predicted that 40% of the Global 2000 enterprises embraced offshore or near-shore IT outsourcing in 2005, and more than 80% of US companies seriously considered outsourcing critical IT services by the end of 2005.
- According to Gartner and IDC, the market for offshore IT services will more than double from about 3% of overall IT services spending in 2005 to between 6% and 7% of overall spending by 2009. Gartner expects offshore IT services to reach $50 billion by 2007. IDC analysts anticipate that the worldwide IT out-

---

[9] Computer Weekly, 17th October 2006.
[10] Computer Weekly, 5th December 2006.

sourcing market will grow to $18 billion by 2008, at an annual compound growth rate of 20%.

- After surveying IT services providers, IDC reported that the offshore component in delivery of US IT services might rise as much as 23% by 2007, up dramatically from 5% in 2003.
- According to IDC, by 2008, nearly one-quarter of US spending on application development, integration and management services will go to offshore providers.
- By 2008, the Global Insight report concluded that IT offshoring will account for roughly $125 billion in additional US Gross Domestic Product (GDP) annually, (a $9 billion jump in real US exports and $250 billion by 2015);
- In the European financial services sector alone, Datamonitor forecasts growth of $240 million in offshore outsourcing during the next 12 to 20 months.
- According to Datamonitor, the Business Process Outsourcing (BPO) market is the single fastest growing area of the IT services sector, growing at a rate of 8% annually. It is estimated to be worth £214 billion today and is predicted to grow to almost £375 billion in 2008.
- According to NASSCOM, the outsourcing market in India was on a dramatic and steady rise – the IT sector was expected to exceed $36 billion in annual revenue in 2005, an increase of 28% and contributing 4.8% of GDP. The sector is on target to achieve $60 billion in export revenue by 2010[11].
- According to NASSCOM, India's outsourcing and back-office services continued its brisk growth. India export revenue was expected to rise above $31 billion in 2006/07. India's average annual growth of 30% in the sector is being driven by Tata Consultancy Services, Infosys Technologies and Wipro. The sector was expected to employ 1.6 million people by March 2007, up from 1.28 million a year earlier. The USA accounted for two thirds of India's exports, the UK contributed 15%, and meanwhile India's domestic information technology market was expected to grow 25% to reach $15.9 billion in the current fiscal year.
- 60% of the Fortune 500 companies outsource to India[12].

Clearly each analyst firm has their own views about the size and growth of the outsourcing market; typically these vary to a large degree. However, what is undeniable is that outsourcing has been and will continue to grow.

Many question the sustainability of the outsourcing model especially as the wage gap between those sending outsourcing services to offshore countries is narrowing. However, an underlying and fundamental demographic difference between the two provides a compelling and long term impetus to a continuing trend for outsourcing.

---

11 NASSCOM McKinsey Report (2005).

12 Veena Jha ed., India & the Doha Work Programme, 147 (2006).

In many western developed countries, the nations are suffering from a demographic squeeze, whereby there is likely to be fewer workers available to support an ageing population. One answer to the problem is immigration, the other is outsourcing work to other people based in another country. The attitudes (especially for politicians) towards outsourcing are far more manageable than attitudes towards immigration.

1.2.3 India as an outsourcing destination

India represents the world's largest democracy, with a population in excess of one billion, with a relatively high level of political risk, together with the ongoing dispute with Pakistan; many had deemed India as a high risk destination. However recent government initiatives, strong economic growth, peace initiatives with its neighbours and its educated workforce (with over 2 million IT graduates each year) and strong IT skill sets, means India is now the preferred choice for outsourcing. India had over 42 IT CMM level 5[13] certified organisations as off 31st March 2002, many Indian Institutes of Technology (IIT) and four equally prestigious Indian Institutes of Management (IIM)[14].

The untapped talent of India was more formally discovered with the advent of the year 2000 problem. India provided the large number of qualified technicians who engaged in the tedious task of reviewing and readjusting many corporate computers.

Information technology is one of the fastest growing sectors in India. The sector witnessed a Compound Annual Growth Rate (CAGR) of 28% from Fy2002[15]. Its share of GDP doubled from 2.9% in Fy2002 to 4.8% in Fy2006. At present the sector is estimated to be US$36.3 billion[16].

The IT segment accounts for a major chunk of the IT-IteS[17] industry in India, with a revenue of US$29.1 billion in Fy2006. Between Fy2002 and Fy2006, the IT segment grew at a CAGR of 25%.

The IteS segment recorded a 45% growth from Fy2002 to Fy2006. The size of the Indian IteS-BPO markets is estimated at US$7.2 billion in Fy2006[18].

India's stock of human capital in terms of qualified people was already one of the highest in the world in 1999 due to high quality tertiary educational institutions.

---

13 Offshore Outsourcing: key commercial and legal issues, Murali Neelakantan.
14 Todd Furniss and Michael Janssen, Offshore Outsourcing Part 1: The Brand of India, April 2003.
15 NASSCOM Strategic Review, 2006.
16 The Economic Times, 7th June 2006.
17 Information Technology Enabled Services.
18 NASSCOM Strategic Review, 2006.

Table 1 below compares the number of graduates in the year.

Table 1. Graduates by country and subject matter

	Natural sciences (Physics, Chemistry, Biology, Mathematics, computer science etc)	Engineering	Total
Global	918	868	1786
EU	182	135	317
USA	144	61	205
China	60	195	255
India	147	29*	176

* This was only the engineering degree holders graduating in 1998. In 2004, the total number of engineering graduates (degree and diploma) was around 350,000.
SOURCE: National Science Foundation, Morgan Stanley Research, Global services sourcing: issues of cost and quality, Nirupam Bajpai, Rohit Arora and Horpreet Khurana; centre of Globalisation and sustainable development; (CSGD Working Paper No 16, June 2004).

In addition, India gains from the fact that a large proportion of the educated workforce can speak English. Every year, India adds about 2.3 million English speaking graduates (15 years education). This compares with around 1.2 million graduates every year in the USA. Going forward the number of engineers (diploma and degree holders) in India is expected to rise sharply. As per NASSCOM, the number of students being admitted for engineering studies in India was to increase to 600,000 in 2004 compared with 455,000 in 2000.

Off special interest is the facilitating legal framework for outsourcing that India provides. Special export processing zones (SEEPZs) and software information technology parks (SITPs) enjoy legal domain benefits and special tax benefits with regard to import duties as well as income taxes. The approved SITPs in India enjoy customs duty-free imports in return for committed exports of IT service. SITPs also enjoy 100% tax holidays on export profits. Under the scheme, IT companies within SITP units are eligible for certain incentives and benefits. In order to claim exemption, the SITP unit must export at least 50% of its total production. Until recently, domestic law stated that a change in control of an SITP unit would result in loss of the tax exemption. This restriction has been discontinued with effect from 1st April 2003. Tax benefits under these parks will however expire in March 2009.

The SEZ Act 2005 came into force in February 2006, since then the government has cleared 150 projects for the setting up of SEZs. Of these:

- 27 SEZs have received the final approval in Andra Pradesh
- 26 have been cleared in Maharastra and
- 20 in Tamil Nadu.

Of the 150 approved SEZs, 85 are dedicated to IT[19].

Research reports on the size of the outsourcing market are plentiful and all point to exponential growth in the volume and value of the outsourcing market. Most highlight India as the preferred destination for outsourcing of key services. However several barriers exist to the achievement of these forecasts. These barriers include:

- Concerns for security of customer and product information.
- The situation with respect to the protection of intellectual property.
- The financial viability of service providers in an increasingly competitive market.
- The ability to provide consistent quality of service.
- The potential for changing nature of local laws.

Having said that, amongst the contenders for leading outsource destinations, India offers a strong value proposition[20]:

1. India offers skilled manpower – the historic British ties mean English speaking manpower is abundant. India also offers a highly qualified and capable workforce.
2. India offers lower HR costs – salary levels in India are around a fifth of the salary levels of developed countries and are typically lower than other outsource destinations. The average salary level for an IT professional is US$ 10,000[21].
3. India offers a well established education and training capability – India has several world renowned universities offering comprehensive technical and business skills. India also has well established industry associations such as NASSCOM, the Federation of Indian Chamber of Commerce and Industry (FICCI), which are actively representing the interests of the Indian service providers.
4. Indian Government support - India has stated its long term objective of being a prime destination of outsourcing services and as such various tax incentives have been made available by Central Government. Furthermore State Governments are actively supporting the outsourcing industry and are implementing favourable policies, such as amending labour laws that are favourable to outsourcing. Central Government has also relaxed foreign direct investment limits, which is bringing about access to increased capital as well as know-how from the developed world.

---

19 Deccan Chronicle, 8^{h} September 2006.

20 Of the financial services firms transferring functions offshore, nearly half are targeting India, which has a huge market of operations and IT professionals earning much lower wages than similarly skilled employees in G7 countries – source: Banking Technology: Outsourcing supplement 2005.

21 Gerhard Rohde, Head of IBITS, UNI-Europe (4th Plenary of the European E-Skills Forum).

5. Improving infrastructure – although historically a distinct disadvantage for India, recent liberalisation measures, especially within the telecommunications field, have seen improved roll-out and quality of infrastructure together with falling prices.
6. Maturity of Indian outsourcing sector – India has a longer history of outsourcing than many other destinations. The experience of the sector has provided a formidable reputation, especially within the software segment.

1.2.4 Destination India

Up until recently, India's outsourcing nerve centres have been in the likes of Bangalore, Mumbai, Delhi, Gurgaon and Noida[22]. Just like in any situation where demand starts to outstrip supply, the economic consequences of increased employment costs, rent etc has meant many outsourcing service providers have started looking beyond these traditional destination centres, to the likes of Pune[23], Chandigarth, Kolkata, Indore, Ahmedabad, Cochin, Chennai, Hyberabad, Jaipur and Rajkot. An increasing problem cited by many service providers in India is the attrition of employees. This not only adds costs, it also leads to a depleting pool of skilled and knowledgeable workforce. However, infrastructure development within tier 2 cities is far behind tier 1 cities and therefore the migration from tier 1 cities to tier 2 cities is likely to be a gradual process.

Apart from workforce costs, the other major cost for service providers is real estate. The real estate market in Tier 1 and Tier 2 cities has being growing fast and increasingly attracting domestic and foreign investors. Indian cities are customary divided into 3 groups:

1. Tier 1 comprises the capital Delhi, the financial centre Mumbai and the IT hub Bangalore.
2. Tier 2 comprise Hyderbad, Pune, Chennai, the cities targeted by companies as alternative offshoring destinations and now possessing a well trained pool of labour.

---

[22] GE Capital employs approx 14,000 in Gurgaon, Bangalore and Hyderbad, Amex employs approx 2,000 in Delhi, Citibank employs approx 4,000 in Mumbai, Standard Chartered employs around 1,000 in Chennai, HSBC employs around 1,500 in Hyderbad, AXA employs around 500 in Bangalore, SwissAir employs around 600 in Mumbai, Lithuania employs around 600 in Delhi, the WorldBank employs around 150 in Chennai, whilst McKinsey employs around 1,500 in Delhi (SOURCE: Avendus Advisors).

[23] Pune is in close proximity to Mumbai, yet is much cheaper in terms of real estate and HR costs. Pune has excellent educational institutions (around 100,000 university graduates each year) and active political support from state government has meant it is now a favourite with BPO suppliers. mSource, Wipro, Infosys Technologies, IBM, Cognizant Technology Solutions, Mahindra British Telecom, HSBC all have centres in Pune for example.

3. Tier 3 cities are usually those with populations in excess of a million, but not completely established as outsourcing and offshoring destinations.

The cost advantage of Tier 2 cities over Tier 1 cities is estimated to be around 20%. Tier 3 cities cost advantage is estimated to be of the order 15-30%[24].

1.2.5 An overview of outsourcing agreements

The foundation of any outsourcing relationship is laid out in an outsourcing agreement. The prime area of importance, from an early stage within any outsourcing agreement is a clear understanding of what services are being outsourced – i.e. the scope of the outsourcing relationship. For an outsourcing relationship to work successfully it is essential to fully understand all the technical, commercial and legal issues of relevance within that relationship. This usually calls for a multi-disciplinary team, consisting of consultants, lawyers, accountants, tax specialists, technology experts, benchmarking experts etc.

For all the hype around outsourcing, historically 70% renegotiate or are unhappy with the relationship within two years. 50% are unhappy within one year. 90% have major issues arising between the parties and 55% have disputes, many of which lead to formal alternative dispute resolution procedures or litigation. 95% of outsourcing relationships end early[25]. In many cases these are due to legitimate reasons, as businesses change their mind or strategic direction, or the scope of the services change or some M&A activity changes the relationship.

The Legal Director / Wraggle and Co benchmark 2003 found that 35% of outsourcing contracts had required substantial mid-term revision and that a quarter of companies polled terminated a contract early. In many cases, issues arise out of a misunderstanding of cultural differences, out of a mistaken attitude towards the relationship – one of different expectations.

An outsourcing agreement forms the core of a successful outsourcing relationship and needs to be drafted meticulously and capture the business strategies and concerns as well as the commercial understanding of the parties.

The agreement should clearly detail the services to be outsourced and the resources to be dedicated in providing the services. The agreement should also have a provision for widening the scope of services and the fees that would be charged for these additional services in the course of the agreement.

One of the most important reasons for outsourcing is to capitalise on the expertise and higher quality of services offered by the service provider. One of the impor-

24 Jones Long Laselle (2005), India the next IT offshoring locations, Tier 3 cities.

25 Simmons and Simmons International Survey, 2005.

tant areas that an agreement should address is related to service levels, such as specifying the deliverables, performances to be measured and methods for measuring service levels, such as the use of benchmarks.

Most outsourcing relationships face problems in relation to: scope creep, cost escalation, technology evolution, lack of pricing granularity, lack of precise service definition, ineffective or un-quantified service levels, feeling of lock-in by the customer, ineffective contract management and more frequently, unstructured governance.

One of the fundamental differences between an outsourcing agreement and other contracts is the length of period the contract lasts. Outsourcing agreements tend to last for several years, sometimes up to ten years. It is impossible for the parties to contemplate all possible eventualities within this period and therefore the contract must allow some flexibility in terms of changing scope, pricing and indeed early contract termination if necessary. Contract termination may be undertaken for a number of reasons; Termination by default – usually a material breach of the contract, or Termination for convenience – usually has an accompanying early termination fee. Under both cases, transition provisions following termination must be carefully thought through, including contractual obligations for continuing service provision and effects of termination on such things as payment of outstanding fees, IP and confidential information and current work orders.

One of the most often cited difficulties in outsourcing and where a large part of the contract agreements focuses, is concerned with Intellectual Property (IP):

- IP owned / licensed by the service provider.
- IP owned / licensed by the customer.
- Developed IP.

Another area where much is cited, especially within the press, is the area of Privacy and Data Protection. The service provider has access to personal and sensitive data of the customer's clients. The customer may be bound by its own contractual conditions or legal obligations to protect the privacy of its clients.

Parties usually have a choice of which country's laws govern an outsourcing agreement, usually either the service provider or customer. It is also in some cases possible to choose the laws of a foreign country that has nexus with the parties or the agreement - however this is not always possible or legally clear.

Laws of foreign jurisdictions may be applicable to a transaction, even if the laws of India govern the agreement. It is imperative that parties to an outsourcing transaction examine issues relating to industry specific regulations of the country in which the company operates.

It is a well known fact that the Indian legal system is slow and sometimes expensive to pursue. With this in mind many outsourcing agreements state an Alternative Dispute Resolution (ADR) process that the parties can follow in the event of a dispute. Such alternatives usually revert to an arbitration process. Arbitration is usually held in accordance with the rules of the International Chamber of Commerce (ICC) or the London Court of International Arbitration (LCIA) for international commercial arbitration.

If there is a dispute between the parties that is subject to arbitration or litigation, the award or decree must be enforced against the losing party. Such enforcement can occur within or outside of India.

- India is a signatory to the New York Convention on the Recognition of "Foreign Arbitral" Awards, 1968 (NYC) and therefore Foreign Awards can be enforced in India.
- Enforcement of "Foreign Judgements" in India is possible - A foreign judgement may be enforced by filing a suit upon judgement under section 13 of the Code of Civil procedure, 1908 (CPC); or by proceedings executed under section 44A of the CPC, provided that the judgement is rendered by a court in a reciprocating territory.

It is clear that in such a complicated relationship with the stakes as high as they are, a straight forward transaction model is likely to prove ineffective in achieving all the aims of both parties over the foreseeable period of the relationship. A partnership model will prove more beneficial to both parties, but what is a partnership model?

Apart from commitment from senior management and open communication channels, such relationships usually have clear delineation of customer and service provider roles and responsibilities. They have services and the service regime properly established, with management tools available to avoid common problematic issues and to keep things in check – usually through good governance. They typically have pricing granularity and financial incentives to behave in a "partnerial" way. They accept change will happen and include balanced and open change control processes which avoid unstructured scope creep. They balance liabilities and iron out termination rights and post termination assistance from the very beginning.

The next chapter delves in a little more detail the concept of outsourcing, the benefits and risks involved and the types of models commonly used in outsourcing.

2. Outsourcing fundamentals

This chapter gives a brief resume of what outsourcing is all about, the different forms, the purported benefits and risks. The chapter also discusses typical contract arrangements, including the separation of transfer of assets and services.

2.1 Purported benefits

There are a number of potential or at least purported benefits which can be achieved through outsourcing. Many commentators have listed these based upon experience from various firms that have gone through the process. However outsourcing is not a homogeneous activity. The benefits from outsourcing depend very much upon which activities are outsourced, the reasons for outsourcing and the specific objectives (these will clearly vary by industry and size of the organisation in question) they have in mind, not to mention the choice of the outsourcing service provider. The typical benefits stated by many authors from outsourcing activity tend to include the following:[26]

- By outsourcing non-value added functions to service providers, it allows further focus of management's effort to the "core" function of the company.
- It allows the achievement of cost-savings by reducing overheads and consequent reduction in training needs for employees. Cost savings will most likely continue as a priority for most outsourcing deals as customers continue to adjust to the challenging economic environment. However recent experience of outsourcing deals, have left customers becoming concerned at mortgaging short term savings for long term losses – customers are increasingly demanding savings as well as protections to ensure that they maintain market rate pricing for the life of the agreement.
- It enables the sharing of cost-savings achieved through economies of scale gained by the outsourcing service provider.

---

[26] Adapted from Outsourcing and Offshoring: Part 1 The Increasing Globalisation of Information Technology Activity, The CIO Summit, Dec7, 2004 by Richard S. Wyde, Davis Wright Tremaine LLP and Outsourcing and Offshoring: Pushing the European Model over the Hill, Rather than off the Cliff, Working paper 05-1, 2005, by Jacob Funk Kirkegaard, Institute of International Economics and Survey of Current & Potential Outsourcing End-Users - The Outsourcing Institute Membership, 1998.

- It allows the achievement of higher levels of service and performance due to specialization of the service provider.
- It potentially allows a reduction of capital expenditure, particularly in the sphere of information technology services, management and general support systems.
- It allows sharing of new and improvements in older technology methods from the service provider to the customer, gained from a combination of specialisation and economies of scale and scope.
- It potentially enables shorter times to market for a customer's services, due to a more flexible and responsive process for the outsourced services.
- Outsourcing provides an opportunity for the customer to standardise its IT infrastructure and to simplify its processes – possibly in a shorter time than it would be feasible without outsourcing.
- It enables an improvement in processes and their documentation – something that tends to get ignored internally, but which takes on an importance on its own right when outsourcing.

Clearly there are many benefits that a properly selected service provider and a managed outsourcing agreement can deliver. Some of which are cost savings and some of which are innovative processes or usage of technology or indeed the skill set of a specialized service provider.

2.2 Costs and risks of outsourcing

However there are a number of costs and risks inherent in outsourcing which need to be assessed and managed. Many of the risks of outsourcing have been highlighted or indeed exaggerated by the press and need to be assessed in the context of the wider benefits achieved through outsourcing and the probability of a firm having to face such a risk.

The typical costs and risks that a customer must access include:

- Loss of day-to to-day management control of outsourced services and excessive dependence on the service provider for performance.
- Dependence on the service provider for strategic information on internal technology, operational and business options.
- By transferring employees and assets to the outsourcing service provider, the customer risks losing valuable knowledge and experience from displaced workers.
- Additional costs associated with managing the outsourcing service provider.
- Reassuming responsibility for the outsourced services on termination of outsourced services can be inherently difficult and risky.

2.3 Outsourcing models

The degree to which the benefits and risks of outsourcing can be managed depends on the model of outsourcing followed. There are essentially four basic forms of outsourcing to India. Each form poses different operational risks for companies:

- Captive Direct – In a captive direct offshoring model, organisations use their own organisation to create an organisation within India, often known as captive centres. Because captive centres require a sizeable upfront investment, only larger companies have the necessary resources to use this model. In theory, captive direct offshoring poses lesser risks to an organisation than any of the other models, because dedicated management from the parent company directly oversees the Indian operations.
- Joint Venture – This model of outsourcing occurs when a domestic firm partners with an Indian entity for shared control of the Indian operations. In general, because control is shared with the foreign enterprise, this method of offshoring has a higher risk potential than the wholly owned foreign captive direct model. However because of the ability to exercise control through majority ownership of the venture (or partial control with a 50 percent or less share of ownership), this form in general, has less risk associated with it than the direct and indirect third-party contracting forms described below.
- Direct Third Party – In the direct third party model, firms outsource operations to a third party service provider located in India. Because the outsourcer has no ownership authority in this form, their control over this working arrangement is limited to the contract terms agreed with the third party service provider, thereby making this model potentially more risky than either the captive or joint venture forms. In some cases the outsourcing customer may elect a build, operate and transfer model, i.e. contracting for services with a third party with an option to acquire the services operation, at some point in time in the future.
- Indirect Third Party – The indirect third party model of offshoring typically occurs when an outsourcer enters into a contract with a domestic outsource service provider, who then subcontracts out all, or a part of the work, to an offshore company. It is quite possible to have a relatively lower risk if the contract is between two domestic companies, as the usual issues of foreign law are not relevant for the outsourcer – essentially the indirect third party bears these risks.

The book concentrates on issues relevant to the latter two forms of outsourcing, as these pose the greatest risk and therefore the formation and agreement of an adequate contract becomes more important. The first two models are essentially in the domain of multinationals or large organisations that should have sufficient finance and skill sets to ensure the adopted model works to their benefit.

2.4 Typical outsourcing arrangements

The outsourcing agreement may be a single, comprehensive document (which may be administratively simpler) or a "master" agreement that includes a process by which specific order forms, statements of work, or other ancillary "sub-agreements" which may be included as needed (which in theory should provide greater flexibility).

Another contractual issue that needs to be determined (especially in the context of multinationals) in the context of an outsourcing model is whether to have a centralized or decentralized approach to contract formation and management.

The decentralized approach uses a master agreement that the parent company of the customer signs with the parent company of the service provider. This master agreement discusses only the principles of the outsourcing transaction. The core issues of scope and pricing form the basis of the local agreements. These contracts are between the customer's local affiliate and the service provider's local office. This can provide more comfort to customers, as local entities may feel more comfortable dealing with local entities, and with local business customs and local laws. The disadvantage is that the parent company has to negotiate a separate agreement in each country. Since there is no central authority, the parent company has to work hard to control the entire relationship.

The alternative is a centralized approach, whereby the master agreement contains all the detail. The local agreements, instead of being robust, just list local topics that are uniquely affected by local law – typically focused around labour laws. However issues of taxation can be a problem since each country has its own rules – currency translation also becomes a factor, since the contract is unwritten in a single currency.

Outsourcing contracts commonly consist of services agreements, supplemented by schedules that describe the services, service level commitments, charges, transitional arrangements and other particulars. Their bulk and complexity resembles a merger or acquisition contract. The challenge to fully document the schedules and other related aspects of the transaction can often be the defining factor between a successful outsourcing arrangement and a deal gone bad.

A service provider will typically advocate that the customer uses the service provider's templates when developing schedules. While the templates may simplify the drafting process, they will generally contain language and legacies preferred by the service provider. It is imperative that templates are properly customized to fit the requirements and content of the particular deal, and balance the power and requirements of both parties and not just the service provider.

The outsourcing lifecycle usually begins with service provider selection and is confirmed by the creation and agreement of a contract. However, what is often overlooked is that the contract is a long term agreement, which needs to specify how the service will be delivered and how the process of regular renegotiation or termination will be managed.

Such agreements are usually long term, (i.e. 5-10 years[27]), because the service provider may be replacing the customer's internal staff, and making significant investments of its own that it intends to recoup over a long period of time. Because of the length of the relationship, it is often difficult to fully anticipate, describe and manage contingencies and change conditions in the agreement. Therefore these agreements often include within the contract, broad procedures that describe the process the parties will follow when changes occur in the relationship, without having to re-write the contract.

A contract can be considered incomplete if it fails to specify performance obligations for the parties in all the different conditions, or fails to specify the nature of the performance itself[28].

The choice of more flexible contracts, which allow adjustment, is the result of a compromise between the advantages of having an open ended agreement and the cost of these flexible contracts[29].

Best business practice appears to use a master agreement so additional services or projects can be performed for the same customer simply by adding an agreed upon statement of work which is signed by both parties[30]. This lowers the cost and reduces the time to document additional deals with the same customer. Any changes in the allocation of risk for a specific project can be made in the applicable statement of work[31].

2.5 Separation of assets and operations

In outsourcing contracts, there are two typical contracts, one for the transfer of existing business (usually assets) and one for the actual services outsourced, as illustrated in Fig 1 below.

---

27 According to HI Europe, the average contract term for IT and business process outsourcing contracts increased from 4.7 years in 1995 to 6.2 years in 2003.

28 Perry, M.K. "Vertical Integration: Determinants and Effects", Handbook of Industrial Organisation, Vol 1, Shmalesnse and Willing Ed, Chapter 4 (1989), 183-255.

29 Crocker, K.J., Masten, S.E., "Pretia Ex Machina? Prices and Process in Long Term Contracts",, Journal of Law and Economics, Vol 34 (1991), 69-100.

30 Elizabeth Sparrow, Successful IT Outsourcing, Springer Verlag (2003).

31 Key Service Agreement Issues: Service Providers Checklist by Fred M. Greguras and David J. Barry, Fenwick & West LLP.

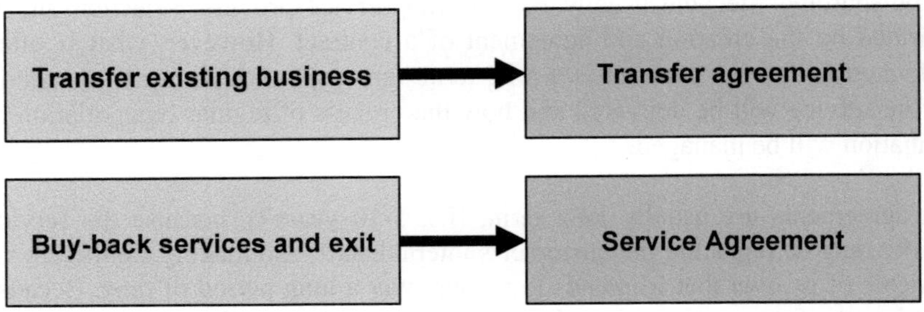

Fig.1. Separation of assets and operations

The "transfer of assets" agreement document, deals with the transfer, where relevant, of any real property, tangible assets, employees and Intellectual Property (IP), (the "Transfer Agreement").

The outsourcing "services agreement" document, is used to record and reflect the service description and service levels in addition to customer and the service provider roles and responsibilities during the term of the outsourcing ("the Service Agreement").

The "Transfer Agreement" usually commences contemporaneously with the agreement and then falls away after effectively establishing the relationship.

2.5.1 Transfer of assets

In order for the outsourcing service provider to perform its services, various assets of the outsourcing customer may need to be transferred to the outsourcing service provider. This transfer of assets is dealt with by a "Transfer Agreement" whereby the IT, employees, IP assets in question, are formally transferred to the outsourcing service provider (independent valuation of these assets may be needed). Assets for such a transfer typically include computer hardware, telecommunications equipment, software licenses, leases on equipment, and various equipment maintenance contracts. For the assignment of leases and contracts from the outsourcing customer to the outsourcing service provider, the consent of third parties may be required.

Software licenses typically include clauses protecting the licenser's proprietary rights. Key software issues in an outsourcing agreement revolve around transferring the customer's software licenses to the service provider for that company's access and use. These licenses may also restrict the scope of the use of the software to the licensee's own internal business. Ideally the customer would have negotiated a clause that contemplated eventual outsourcing of its service and software.

In some cases, a third party software vendor will not give consent to an assignment without the payment of a substantial extra fee. Most software suppliers tend to treat an assignment in the same way as the granting of a new license and thus will demand the payment of the full licensing fee, which may be substantial. It is therefore important to ascertain in the "Transfer of Asset" agreement the allocation of costs involved in carrying out the necessary transfer of assets.

In many cases, for confidentiality reasons, the parties will not seek the third party consent or waivers until all the issues between the parties have been resolved and the outsourcing agreement is ready to be signed. This however means the software licenser has significant power, which leads to heated negotiations between the parties and the software licenser.

In the UK, transfer of assets may be liable to value added taxation and stamp duty. This hidden cost of the "Transfer of Assets" agreement has to be taken into account in the overall outsourcing consideration, and companies based in countries outside the UK should enquire the position within their own country.

2.5.2 Transfer of staff

A common feature for many outsourcing agreements is the "transfer of staff" from the outsourcing customer to the outsourcing service provider. In the EU, labour regulations (such as the EU acquired Rights Directive 77/187/EEC), require elaborated procedures to be completed before the staff transfer can take place and their existing terms of services need to be guaranteed in the transfer.

For complete outsourcing involving the wholesale transfer of an in-house IT function to an outsourcing service, the UK situation appears to be that the above regulations are likely to apply[32]. It is however not entirely clear whether the above regulations apply in the UK for limited outsourcing arrangements involving transfer of only a part of the IT function of the customer to the service provider – similar considerations will need to be considered for companies based outside the UK.

Since the outsourcing service provider, who is obliged to take on the transferred employees, will have to pay the same staff costs and these costs will most probably be passed on to the outsourcing customer in the negotiation of pricing of the outsourcing contract, the net saving of staff costs expected in an outsourcing arrangement of this sort may be difficult to realize.

[32] Kenny v South Manchester College, 1993, IRLR 265.

2.5.3 Service Agreement

The Service Agreement is the core of the outsourcing agreement, it defines the services that are to be outsourced, the processes that will be followed and the pricing and SLA's associated with such services. The Service Agreement may include a transition-in plan which enables the services and the SLAs to be fine tuned before the core service agreement kicks-in. In addition the various legal relationships and obligations, the protection of IP and conformance to Data Privacy are all matters dealt with within the Services Agreement.

The next chapter discusses the common attitudes to outsourcing and how these may affect the outsourcing process.

3. Attitudes to outsourcing worldwide

Outsourcing is not entirely new: in 1985 Opel Cars in Germany outsourced the entire IT operations to EDS. In 1989, Kodak shifted its IT to IBM.

Outsourcing for manufacturing of products has been established for decades, with the likes of "Nike" outsourcing the production of trainers to cheaper countries, such as India, China and Bangladesh. Then a wave of IT outsourcing took effect, which included basic labour intensive functions such as data entry, data processing, programming and IT support, driven to a large extent by the Y2K problems. Now the wave of outsourcing seems to have moved into the area of BPO. Figure 2 below illustrates the evolution of outsourcing services over time.

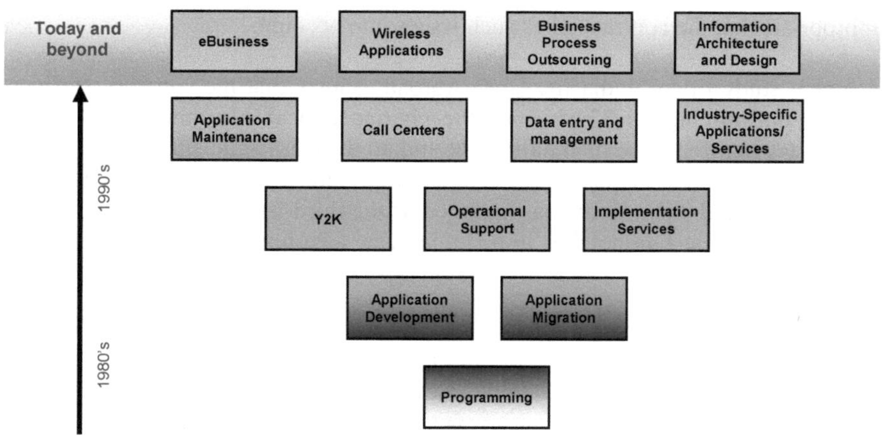

Fig. 2. Evolution of outsourcing services over time

Although outsourcing and offshoring clearly presents cost advantages for those that outsource. This cost advantage is not always passed onto the end-user and as such the benefits from outsourcing is not always recognized at the public level. What however does seem to make the headlines is the negative reporting about outsourcing / offshoring, particularly with respect to lost jobs at the domestic level. An Associated Press poll in May 2004 found that 69% of Americans believe outsourcing hurts the US economy. An Employment Law Alliance poll taken the same month found that 58% of American workers believe that the Federal government should penalize companies that offshore work. Research from Deloitte and Touche found that a mere 4% of Britons support the continuation of offshoring, while a third believe that UK companies should be forced to bring jobs back to the UK.

Attitudes to outsourcing tend to be strongly led by the actions of governments. Most European countries are a little behind the USA and UK in their adoption of and attitude to outsourcing. Many European countries still see outsourcing as a cost-cutting exercise, which creates a negative reaction towards outsourcing. More fundamental is the general attitude towards free markets and globalisation. Many countries are still much more pro-closed economies, preferring trading with local companies than international firms.

Within this context, it is important that parties are fully cognisant of attitudes towards outsourcing within their countries and would be wise to ensure an appropriate PR initiative which demonstrates the benefits of the company outsourcing to the local economy is an integral part of the outsourcing process and possibly the negotiation process. With the background of negative sentiment towards outsourcing, a small failure on the part of the service provider is likely to result in a disproportionate effect upon the customer and its public image. It may therefore be appropriate that the contract takes such issues into account.

A recent study titled "India Inc Goes Abroad" shows that the software Business process outsourcing (at 33.6%) and the pharmaceutical / healthcare (at 20.5%) sectors account for more than half of the Indian overseas acquisitions. The largest proportion of Indian acquisitions, have been in Europe (around 40%) and North America (around 34%). India has emerged as the third largest investor in the UK, raising its rank by five notches in a single year. Perhaps the sentiment towards outsourcing and lost jobs needs to be put into perspective.

The next chapter looks at the first step within the outsourcing lifecycle, that of service provider selection. It describes the RFP process and how to use it to gauge the likely attitude of the service provider.

4. Selecting an outsourcing service provider

This chapter discusses the process of selecting a suitable service provider and lists the factors that must be assessed as part of a due-diligence exercise.

4.1 Minimising risks through the choice of an appropriate service provider

Selecting an outsourcing service provider is both a time consuming and challenging task for any customer, more so for those contemplating outsourcing for the first time and even more so for those with limited resources, such as SMEs.

It is absolutely essential to ensure the team that is assembled to undertake the task of outsourcing and selecting a service provider consists of all the appropriate skills and experience that such a complex task demands. More often than not, customers assign the task to an IT department manager or technology manager. Usually such departments are not the end users or process managers and as such, the choice of a service provider is based upon the decision of neither the end-user or the process owner or in fact someone with sufficient financial / commercial or legal knowledge to be reasonably confident the service provider will be able to deliver upon the objectives of the customer.

Booz Allen Hamilton undertook a survey[33] of 158 executives from companies across a range of industries involved in defining and managing their company's outsourcing strategies. The survey identified the top three evaluation factors considered when selecting an outsourcing service provider as being:

1. Capabilities of the service provider and the quality of services provided
2. Pricing of services and cost savings passed onto the customer; and
3. The service provider's security capabilities and track record in this regard.

Geographic factors were considered the least important decision factor.

---

[33] Outsource Security: Concerns Growing – outsourcing security survey findings, Booz Allen Hamilton, 21st March 2006.

The survey found the four most important cited outsourcing risks by customers as being:

1. Disruptions in product delivery or service caused by breakdown in mission critical business processes or functions.
2. Loss of customer trust or relationships due to improper or fraudulent use of confidential customer data.
3. Loss of intellectual property or other sensitive information via accidental exposure, theft or misuse of corporate data.
4. Brand or reputation damage that results in loss of goodwill arising from actual or perceived risk of security failures.

The survey also found that companies are more concerned about cyber threats than physical breaches and natural disasters – off these the key factor appears to be "theft, misuse or damage of company systems and data from outside the outsourcing service provider".

The survey found that providers with operations in India were perceived to have a relatively high risk factor in terms of the legal and regulatory frameworks within the country. This risk was ranked lower than many other Asian and South American countries, but behind the Emerging EU countries and Western countries.

Of the surveyed companies, it would appear that most want site visits and in-person audits of service provider security procedures and capabilities, followed by references from other clients and 3rd party security certifications (e.g. NASSCOM) for reassurance.

The critical factor for a customer is to ensure a proper and thorough due diligence is undertaken. Careful due diligence must be done on potential service providers in terms of financial stability, employee mobility, intellectual property protection and performance on similar projects.

Useful areas to evaluate and questions to ask include:

Financial status

- What is the financial record and current status of the service provider, especially in relation to the size of the outsourcing deal?
- Is there risk of the service provider ceasing business operations?
- Can the service provider finance asset acquisitions?

Performance record

- What similar projects has the service provider performed?
- Does the service provider have a speciality or niche that is hard to find?
- What do customer references say about quality of work, protection of IP and employee mobility?
- Can the service provider guarantee that employees which are assigned to the customer project, will not churn to another project or competing service provider within certain duration of the agreement?
- What metrics will be used to measure performance of the service provider?
- Does the service provider have quality process certificates?
- What is the size of the company in terms of number of employees?
- What are the service provider's procedures for protecting the IP of its customers?
- What are the service provider's operational procedures and technical safeguards for handling confidential information and or IP?
- Is English language capability required for the service delivery, if so what is the service provider's track record in this regard?

Location / Infrastructure

- Does the location where the work will be performed have adequate infrastructure for telephony services, data communications etc?
- Does the location have a qualified labour pool and what is the workforce mobility rate?

Legal and Regulatory compliance

- Legal systems for the country – does the legal system within the country provide reassurance?
- Are there sufficient statutes and case law around that protect the typical concerns within outsourcing agreements, such as contract enforcement, Intellectual property, Data protection etc?
- Are there any legal cases pending?

Account Management

- Does the service provider have a good track record with respect to account management and responsiveness to customer needs?
- Will the service provider provide a dedicated account manager?
- Does the service provider commit to providing senior management involvement?
- What dispute resolution procedures does the service provider offer?

Innovation

- Does the service provider have products / service which represent innovations with respect to current procedures?
- Does the service provider have a track record of innovation e.g. number of patents filed etc?

Security procedures

- Does the service provider have documented security procedures?
- Is the service provider accredited by an organisation with respect to its security procedures?
- Has the service provider had a history or incidents of lapses in security in the past?

4.2 Service provider challenges from a customer perspective

What many people tend to ignore is the fact that outsourcing agreements are deals between two parties, each with its own set of expectations. Typically it is assumed that outsourcing failures or difficulties arise due to problems created by or misunderstanding by the service provider. Often it is a failure of the customer to clearly define or set appropriate expectations at the outset that lead to many of the problems within such relationships. Internal political interference or power plays within a customer organisation can have the effect of creating poor decision making and poor communication between the customer and service provider. A survey undertaken by Diamond Cluster in 2005, called "Outsourcing Study" found 14 challenges that service providers face when dealing with customers[34], these include:

1. Unrealistic financial expectations.
2. Lack of clear directive.
3. Poor decision making.
4. Poor project management.
5. Low executive commitment.
6. Inadequate skill proficiency and experience.
7. Conflicting communications styles.
8. Stability of technical infrastructure.
9. Anti-outsourcing sentiments.
10. Mismanagement of their own attrition.
11. Misunderstanding regarding capital investment requirements.
12. Poor quality assurance and control.

---

[34] Source: Diamond Cluster 2005, outsourcing study.

13. Lack of professionalism.
14. Conflicting work-style, holiday schedules etc.

Clearly the scope for disagreements to arise during the course of an outsourcing agreement is significant, especially if the internal commitment and processes within the customer have not been fully aligned. It is usually wise to have a single point of contact within the customer organisation which liases with the service provider on a day to day basis, to avoid such a possibility.

It is also essential for both parties to be fully aware of the issue each other faces and understand each other's expectations, limitations and the extent of commitment before deciding whether the parties should tie the knot and sign on the provincial "dotted line".

The first place to start is during the RFP process. Typically, many parties treat the RFP process as simply a gating process and use standard boiler plate templates, without putting in the necessary level of effort to use the process as joint learning exercises, as well as forming a solid basis upon which a contract can be created, should that be the desired intention of the parties. Think of it as a dating game, where the service provider attempts to woo the customer, however the analogy unfortunately doesn't go as far as the old saying that opposites attract!

4.3 The RFP process

Before reaching the contract negotiation stage, various activities need to be performed by the customer. The typical process for contracting with a service provider includes:

1. Identifying requirements – prioritised list of objectives for outsourcing.
2. Preparing and distributing a request for proposal (RFP) – preparing a request for specific requirements that potential interested parties can respond against.
3. Examining proposals.
4. Evaluating service providers – experience, financial standing, management experience etc.
5. Negotiating contracts – critical for ensuring success during and after the term of the agreement.
6. Implementing the outsourcing agreement.

Outsourcing transactions can often take many months to negotiate. The key to avoid drawn out negotiations is to create a structured timeline and procedures for conducting negotiations. The first step in laying the groundwork for a quick negotiation is the preparation of a very detailed, well thought out RFP.

Outsourcing negotiations are often protracted because confusion arises around the types and levels of services that the customer expects the service provider to provide. Drafting an RFP should include business, technical and legal personnel. Legal counsel should be used in describing the services as they could be used as the statement of work exhibit to the actual outsourcing contract.

Typical Request for Proposal (RFP) should include:

- Section 1 – Introduction and overview
  - Introduction
    1. Objective of the RFP – *broad description of the key objectives the customer is seeking*
    2. Services (and statement of work for additional services to be provided by the service provider) – *extensive list of services that the customer wishes to outsource – this should include those that are essential and those which the customer may wish to learn more about from the service provider, but which may not be contracted for, within this specific RFP*
  - Terms and conditions
    3. Jurisdiction – *statement of the jurisdiction for contract performance and enforcement*
    4. Right to clarify – *process (and contact) that interested parties must follow if further clarification is required*
    5. Reimbursement and risk – *statement that the costs of responding to the RFP must be borne by the interested party and risks of late submission of responses would mean disqualification*
    6. Proposal acceptance – *mechanism that the customer will follow in choosing and accepting a formal response by a particular service provider – this may include the fact that the customer may not necessarily choose a submission which is the lowest cost, but one that balances cost with a technical evaluation of the service provider*
    7. Negotiation with bidders – *statement about the right of the customer to negotiate with certain bidders, which may have qualified a specific threshold*
    8. Authority to sign – *statement that proposals must be signed by a legal representative of the service provider, and a statement that such a person signing has the relevant power of attorney to do so*
    9. Late submission – *statement that late submissions will be rejected without being opened*
    10. Copying of responses – *where there is a request for more than one copy of the proposal, the customer may seek that each of the copies is also signed or initialled by the legal representative of the company*
    11. Selection of proposal – *the process that will be followed and possibly the evaluation criteria that will be employed in selection of the best proposal*
    12. Explanation of decision – *statement of the legal obligations or lack off such obligation upon the customer to explain its decision*

13. Improper influence – *statement of the fact that the customer may disqualify any service provider where there is evidence that improper influence has been exercised, this may include bribery, inside knowledge or collusion for instance*
14. RFP communication – *statement of the mechanism that must be employed for communication from the service provider to the customer, points of contact, requirements for all communication to be put in writing and the possibility that any questions in relation to the RFP may be made public*
15. Visit to service provider site – *a statement that a site visit may be necessary as part of the selection process and a placement of an obligation upon the service provider to arrange what may be necessary for this to happen*
16. Requirements reservation – *statement that the customer may seek further clarification*

- Service Provider instruction
17. Communication of intent
18. RFP process schedule
19. RFP response format
20. Initial response
21. Final response
22. Pricing

- RFP evaluation criteria

• Section 2 – Request For Proposal Questionnaire

- Overview of service provider organisation
1. Corporate overview
2. Financials for the past three years including audited accounts
3. Service capability overview
4. Human resources overview, including staff attrition
5. Intellectual property management and protection regime
6. Legal and regulatory history

- Service delivery
7. Staffing for services
8. Relationship management
9. Solution delivery and management overview
10. Proposal delivery model
11. Security and data protection regime
12. Business continuity / disaster recovery
13. Transition planning (in and out)
14. Service level management and reporting
15. Value added services
16. Pricing

- List of appendices
17. Appendix A – about company – brochures etc
18. Appendix B – Service "A" details
19. Appendix C – Service "B" details
20. Appendix D – Service "C" details

21. Appendix E – Indicative Service Levels and Reporting
22. Appendix F – Bidder Worksheet – format of pricing response including fixed and variable elements
23. Appendix G – RFP response format

- Model Agreement – *containing all of the documentation that will be required to complete the outsourcing transaction, including the terms and conditions, the statement of work and the format of the pricing schedule*

The approach the service provider brings to the table in negotiating the terms and conditions may be a test of the approach that it may bring in dealing with problems that will arise during the term of the deal. Customers should be willing to test the level of disagreement in a setting where the consequences of not seeing eye-to-eye are relatively insignificant before signing on the dotted line.

A technique that some customers employ is the use of a "term sheet" approach during negotiations with the service provider. The term sheet process is nothing more than a condensed version of the outsourcing agreement in a table format. It enables both parties to compartmentalise issues and concepts and puts the service provider to a second round of "I agree" or I "Disagree" responses in a live face to face session.

It is always recommended that the customer negotiates with at least two service providers and let both parties know that they face competition. Dual track negotiations allow customers to get a real time comparison of the legal differences between two organisations that will be transposed to the outsourcing agreement. Sometimes a seemingly well priced deal by one service provider is clawed back by legal positions in the agreement that shift too much risk back to the customer.

This brief overview has demonstrated that outsourcing is inherently a complex process where various legal issues need to be given careful and thorough due consideration. However, outsourcing to service providers based in India itself brings additional legal factors that complicate matters further.

It is imperative to understand the legal environment in India before companies contemplate outsourcing to India. Although there is much in common between India and the Western world; indeed much can be learnt from the history and experiences of India, concerns remain in relation to the adequacy of the Indian legal system. The next chapter discusses the Indian legal system in a little more detail.

5. The Indian judicial system

The chapter provides a brief history of India and its laws, looking at the primary and secondary sources of legislation, how the laws are interpreted and how local customs play an important role.

5.1 Primary source of law

The principle of independence of the judiciary is a basic tenant of the Indian Constitution. The Constitution is a written document; the fundamental law of the land, which declares India to be a socialist, secular, democratic republic having a quassi federal structure.

All laws can be grouped into two categories: civil and criminal laws. The Supreme Court and the High courts are known as "Higher judiciary" or "Union judiciary". The other courts are known as "Subordinate courts" or "State judiciary". Besides these, special courts and tribunals are set up for specific purposes.

Legislative power of Parliament and State[35] legislatures are conferred and distributed by Article 246 and List-I, II and III in the Seventh Schedule of the Constitution.

Under List-I, States have exclusive power for enactment of the law with refernact subjects of the State. List II provides that Parliament and State legislatures both have power to make laws, whilst List II is a concurrent list.

A law made by a State legislature with respect to a matter in the concurrent list if repugnant to a law made by Parliament will be void to the extent of the repug-

---

[35] There are 29 States in India, 18 official languages and 1600 dialects. States include: Andhra Pradesh , Arunachal Pradesh , Assam, Bihar, Chhattisgarh, Goa, Gujarat, Haryana, Himachal Pradesh, Jammu and Kashmir, Jharkhand, Karnataka, Kerala, Madhya Pradesh, Maharashtra, Manipur, Meghalaya, Mizoram, Nagaland, Orissa, Punjab, Rajasthan, Sikkim, Tamil Nadu, Tripura, Uttarakhand, Uttar Pradesh, West Bengal, whilst Andaman and Nicobar Islands, Chandigarh, Dadra and Nagar Haveli, National Capital Territory of Delhi, Daman and Diu, Lakshadweep and Pondicherry.

nancy, unless State law received the assent of the President[36] in which case it will prevail in the State.

The primary source of law in India is through the enactments passed by the Parliament. In addition to these, the President of India and the Governor[37] of each State have limited powers to issue ordinances when the Parliament is not in session.

Most enactments delegate powers to the executive to make rules and regulations for the purposes of the Acts. These rules and regulations are periodically laid before the legislature (Union or State as the case may be). This subordinate legislation is another source of law.

5.2 Secondary source of law

An important secondary source of law is the judgments of the Supreme Court, High Court and some of the specialised Tribunals. The judgments of these institutions not only decide legal and factual issues in dispute between the parties but in the process interpret/declare the law. This ratio decidendi is a binding precedent.

The Constitution[38] provides that the law declared by the Supreme Court shall be binding on all courts within India. The ratio decidendi of the Supreme Court constitute binding precedents to be followed by all the other courts and tribunals. The Supreme Court is not bound by its own decisions. However decisions of a larger bench of the Supreme Court are binding on benches of equal or lesser strength.

---

36 Being the head of government of India, the President has exclusive and wide remitting powers, akin to the head of State in the UK, rather than the President of USA. The President however is bound to act on the advice of the council of ministers. The president has executive power, legislative power, monetary powers especially in terms of the national budget, judicial powers in terms of appointment of judges and ratifying rules of procedure decided by Supreme courts, and finally power of emergency.

37 The Governors and Lieutenant-Governors of the states and territories of India have similar powers and functions at the state level as that of the President of India at Union level. The Governor enjoys many different types of powers: Executive powers related to administration, appointments and removals, Legislative powers related to lawmaking and the state legislature, Discretionary powers to be carried out according to the discretion of the Governor. A bill that the state legislature has passed can become a law only after the Governor gives his assent to it. He can return a bill to the state legislature, if it is not a money bill for reconsideration. However, if the state legislature sends it back to him for the second time, he has to give his assent to it. The Governor has the power to reserve certain bills for the President. When the state legislature is not in session and the Governor considers it necessary to have a law, then he can promulgate ordinances.

38 Of India.

Judgments of specialised tribunals are binding on itself but not on the courts or other tribunals.

The Privy Council in London was the highest appellate body for India prior to independence. Judgments of the Privy Council rendered prior to independence are binding precedents unless overruled by the Supreme Court. Decisions of all other foreign courts are only of persuasive value.

5.3 Tribunals

In India, Tribunals are formed according to Art 323B of the Constitution of India and are empowered to decide disputes following the legal procedures. Tribunals are formed to assist the judiciary and to avoid slow, expensive and complex formalities.

Protection and judicial enforcement of Intellectual Property Right, (IPR) are possible both under the statute and under the common law. The statutory remedies of IPR are enforced through specialized IP Tribunals and Courts. The Tribunals have no power to administer equitable remedies or common law remedy since Tribunals are strictly not Courts but have only the trappings of Courts. Law Courts in India, on the other hand, can grant both equitable remedy and statutory remedy[39].

5.3.1 Customs

One of the other important sources of law is local customs. Custom is an unwritten law which expresses doctrine of justice and utility in the society. Family laws such as the Hindu Law or Muslim Law are enacted on the basis of tradition and one should be aware of the differences in customs and its implication upon the law and its interpretation.

5.3.2 Interpretation

In the process of interpretation of Indian statutes, liberal use of foreign decisions of countries following the same system of jurisprudence has been permitted in practice in Indian courts. The help of such decisions is subject to qualification that prime importance is always given to the language of the concerned Indian statute, the circumstances and the setting in which it is enacted and the Indian condition where it is applied – statutory construction must be consistent with Indian philosophy, even if it is based on foreign ideology.

---

[39] Kihota Hollohon v Zachillhu AIR 1993 SC 412 and Sarojani Remaswami v Union of India AIR 1992 SC 2219.

Where the general rule in Indian Code is based on English principle, the Indian courts frequently use the help of English decisions to support the conclusion they reached – generally wherever an Indian Act is based in the model of an English Act, decisions interpreting the provisions of the English Act are referred to as helpful guides for interpreting corresponding provisions of the Indian Act.

Along the connection with the English common law and jurisprudence and similarity of political thoughts, the use of English language as authorative text of Indian statute is another factor which obliges the Indian courts in taking help from foreign precedents of English speaking countries.

The next chapter goes to the heart of the outsourcing agreement, examines critical jurisdiction issues and the laws governing the contract.

6. Critical contract considerations – jurisdiction issues

This chapter discusses the implications of having potentially two different laws affecting the contract and analyses which laws apply under which circumstances. The chapter also introduces "arbitration" as a means of avoiding expensive courtroom litigation and the enforceability of foreign judgments and arbitration awards in India.

6.1 Two systems of law

When contracts transcend national boundaries, the national legal regime of any single country becomes inadequate. When the parties to the contract are located in different countries, at least two systems of law impinge upon the transaction and the rules of International Law come into play.

Whilst the legal environment in India is welcoming for foreign investment and business, with a strong legal system based on English common law that recognises the rule of law and principles of natural justice, due consideration must be given to the legal, regulatory and cultural issues that arise when conducting business in India.

6.2 European legal landscape (common law v's civil law)

Indian law is based upon common law and therefore has much in common with the legal systems of the UK and USA. Although historically there were wide differences between common law and civil law jurisdictions, these distinctions are slowly blurring. However, it is still useful to examine briefly the issues relevant to such legal systems.

Civil law was primarily developed out of the Roman Law of Justinian's Corpus Juris Civilis. Common law originally developed under the inquisitorial system in England from Judicial decisions that were based in tradition, custom and precedent. The difference between civil law and common law lies in the fact that:

- Civil law is codified.
- Civil law is seen as the primarily source of default.
- Common law is based on cases as the primary source of law, while statutes are only seen as incursions into the common law and thus interpreted narrowly.

However, the difference between civil and common law systems is blurring, with the growing importance of jurisprudence in civil law countries and the growing importance of statutes law and codes in common law countries.

6.2.1 Common law countries

Common law constitutes the basis of the legal systems of:

- Australia.
- Brunei.
- England, Wales, Northern Ireland and the Republic of Ireland.
- Federal law of Canada and Provinces (except Qubec).
- Federal law of USA and State laws (except Louisana).
- Hong Kong.
- Malaysia.
- Malta.
- New Zealand.
- Pakistan.
- South Africa.
- Singapore.
- Sri Lanka and many other English speaking countries in the Commonwealth.

India's system of common law is a mixture of English law and local Hindu Law.

6.2.2 Civil law countries

Civil law is not necessarily a homogenous concept, although share many common elements, such as codification and primacy. The following list illustrates the main forms of civil law:

- French civil law – which includes France, Benelux countries, Italy, Spain and the former colonies of these countries.
- German civil law – which includes Germany, Austria, Switzerland, Greece, Portugal, Turkey, Japan, South Korea and the Republic of China.
- Scandinavian civil law – which includes Denmark, Norway, Sweden, Finland and Iceland.

Chinese law is a mixture of civil law and socialist law. The Dutch law cannot be easily placed into one of the systems. The present Russian civil code is in part a translation of the Dutch law.

6.3 Indian contract law

Under Indian Law, execution of decrees, whether foreign or domestic, is governed by the provisions of the Code of Civil Procedure, 1908 (CPC) (as amended from time to time). Sections 13 and 14 enact a rule of res judicata in case of foreign judgments[40].

Under Indian Law, parties are free to stipulate their terms of contract and lay down the law by which the contract[41] is to be governed. Indian Courts follow customary Private International law rules[42]. Choice of law made by parties is acceptable, such as a neutral law. Parties may also choose jurisdiction of courts.

"Choice of law rules" helps to decide which law is applicable to the case[43]. These rules refer to connecting factors[44].

European companies can rely upon the Rome Convention, 1980, which provides that the contracting parties are free to choose the legal system of the contracting state that will govern their contracts. The only requirement is that the choice must be explained or demonstrated with reasonable certainty by the terms of the contract or the circumstances of the case. By their choice, the parties can select the law applicable to the whole or only to a part of the contract (Article 3(1)). It is only in the absence of such choice that the contract will be governed by the law of the country with which it is most closely connected (Article (4)).

---

40 Latin for "the thing has been judged," meaning the issue before the court has already been decided by another court, between the same parties.

41 The Indian Contract Act extends to the whole of India and it came into force on the first day of September 1872. For the formation of a contract there must be a) an agreement b) the agreement should be enforceable by law. The Supreme Court confirmed this in Modi Entertainment Network v. W.S.G. Cricket PTE Ltd. AIR 2003 SC 1177.

42 Private International Law is the law which regulates which courts should take charge, which law should apply and whether judgments should be recognised and enforced across borders in cases with an international dimension. It also includes mechanisms for co-operation and exchange of information between governments and courts in different countries, where these are designed to support mutual recognition of each other's laws and judgments.

43 Set of rules to guide the choice of law to be applied in any given situation will be the proper law. The proper law is the primary law which governs most aspects of the factual situation giving rise to the dispute.

44 The closest and most real connection to the facts of the case - Raiffeisen Zentralbank Osterreich AG v Five Star Trading LLC [2001] EWCA Civ 68, [2001] 2 WLR 1344, [2001] 3 ALL ER 257.

Since India is a common law country, Indian courts take into account considerations similar to those that courts in the UK consider. Typically, courts exercise jurisdiction based on certain rules and these rules are different for civil and criminal causes of action. The rules prescribing the jurisdiction for a civil offence depend on a number of factors depending on whether the offence is characterised as a tort (a civil wrong), as statutory offence, or a contractual breach.

The law specified in the contract usually governs contractual offences. In the absence of a chosen law, the law of the state that has the closest connection to the transaction is usually applied. The "closest connection" is determined by looking at a number of factors including the following:

- The place of contracting.
- The place of negotiation.
- The place of performance.
- The location of the subject matter.
- The currency of payment.
- The domicile, residence, nationality, place of incorporation or place of business of the contracting parties.

Indian law does not specifically address jurisdiction issues related to the Internet. Courts generally use existing principles to determine whether they have jurisdiction over a particular transaction. The Information and Technology Act 2000 is based on the Model Law on E-Commerce adopted by the United Nations Commission on International Trade Law (UNCITRAL), the Singapore Electronic Transactions Act, 1998 and the Malaysian Electronic Signatures Act, however goes to some length to enable e-commerce.

Under the India Contract Act, 1872, contracts are binding irrespective of their form. Therefore unless a specific form is proscribed a contract is binding whether it is oral or in another form, however in some cases, Indian law requires certain documents (and contracts) to be signed by the contracting parties. The basic purpose of a signature is to authenticate a document and to identify and bind the person who signs the document.

The essence of the Information and Technology Act 200 is captured in the long title of the Act, "An act to provide for the legal recognition of transactions carried out by ... alternatives to paper based methods of communication and storage of information..."

The Act comprises of three significant aspects:

- Legal recognition of electronic records and communications - contractual framework, evidentiary aspects, digital signatures as the method of authentication, rules for determining time and place of dispatch and receipt of electronic records.

- Regulation of Certification Authorities ("CAs").
- Cyber contraventions - civil and criminal violations, penalties, establishment of the Adjudicating Authority and the Cyber Regulatory Appellate Tribunal.

The main elements of the Act include:

- Chapter I relates to digital signatures
- Chapter III – electronic governance, gives legal validity to information provided in electronic form, legal recognition of digital signatures
- Chapter IV - scheme for Regulation of Certifying Authorities
- Chapter VII - scheme of things relating to Digital Signature Certificates
- Chapter IX - penalties and adjudication for various offences – tampering with source code, hacking, transmission of obscene information.

The Information and Technology Act, 2000 states that unless otherwise agreed by the parties, an offer and the acceptance of an offer may be expressed by means of "electronic records".

It is also possible to split a contract, to allow different parts to be governed by different laws – where there is an absence of choice, courts determine "proper law" of contract i.e. law with the closest connection to the transaction[45].

It is imperative for European companies to ensure that the parties expressly agree the European law for contract enforcement. An agreement that allows suits relating to disputes within India to be filed in a court in a foreign country[46] is not void. However it cannot deprive an Indian court from exercising its jurisdiction. The court in India can adjudicate such a suit if it considers that the ends of justice will be better served by the trial of the suit of India. To determine this, the court will

[45] The best way to ensure the application of a particular legal system to international contracts is to choose a particular law to govern the contract. This law is called the "Proper Law of the Contract". Sections 13, 15 and 44A of the Indian Code of Civil Procedure and Section 41 of the Indian Evidence Act, govern the conclusiveness and enforcement of foreign judgments in India. If there is a reciprocal arrangement between India and the foreign country whose judgment is sought to be enforced, then under section 44A of the Indian Code of Civil Procedure, the said foreign Decree could be executed as if it were a Decree passed by the Indian court without the need to file a Suit. If there is no reciprocal arrangement between the foreign country concerned and India, then the said Judgment/ Decree can be enforced in India by filing a Suit on the foreign judgment. A bare statement of a court is not enough. There should be an express exclusion of the jurisdiction of all other courts, Naziruddian v. P.A Annamalai, AIR 1978 Mad 410.

[46] A Foreign Court is defined as a court situated outside India and not established or continued by the authority of the Central Government. A Foreign Judgment means a judgment of a Foreign Court.

look into the balance of convenience, the interests of justice and the circumstances of the case[47].

To exercise jurisdiction, there must first exist "jurisdiction to prescribe." Assuming jurisdiction to prescribe exists, "jurisdiction to adjudicate" and, "jurisdiction to enforce" need to be examined. The foregoing three types of jurisdiction are often interdependent and based on similar considerations.

6.4 Jurisdiction to prescribe

"Jurisdiction to prescribe" means that the substantive laws of the forum country are applicable to the particular persons and circumstances.

Under international law, there are six generally accepted bases of jurisdiction under which a country may claim to have jurisdiction to prescribe a rule of law over an activity[48]. In the context of outsourcing contracts, the following are key:

1. Subjective Territoriality - conduct that, wholly or in substantial part, takes place within its territory.
2. Objective Territoriality - conduct outside its territory that has or is intended to have substantial effect within its territory.
3. Nationality - the activities, interests, status, or relations of its nationals outside as well as within its territory.

Cutting across the foregoing criteria of international law is a general requirement of reasonableness. Thus, even when one of the foregoing bases of prescriptive jurisdiction is present, a country may not exercise jurisdiction to prescribe law with respect to a person or activity having connection with another country if the exercise of jurisdiction would be unreasonable[49].

6.5 Jurisdiction to adjudicate

Jurisdiction to adjudicate means that the tribunals of a given country may resolve a dispute in respect to a person or thing where the country has jurisdiction to prescribe the law that is sought to be enforced.

---

47 U.L Lastochkina v Union of India, AIR 1976 AP 103.

48 Darrel Menthe, Jurisdiction in Cyberspace: A theory of international spaces, 4 Mich. Telecomm. Tech. L. Rev 69 (1998).

49 G. Born, Reflections on Judicial Jurisdiction in International Cases, 17 GA. J. Int. & Comp. Law 1, 33 (1987); and Asahi Metal Indus. Co. v. Superior Court, 480 U.S. 102, 115 (1987).

6.6 Jurisdiction to enforce

A country may employ judicial or non-judicial measures to induce or compel compliance or punish non-compliance with its laws or regulations, provided it has jurisdiction to prescribe. Thus, a country may not exercise authority to enforce law that it had no jurisdiction to prescribe.

While jurisdiction to prescribe can be extraterritorial and jurisdiction to adjudicate can also extend to persons outside the territory of the adjudicating entity, jurisdiction to enforce is strictly territorial[50]. One country may not enforce its criminal law in another country's territory without the latter country's consent. The same is essentially true of the enforcement of civil law. Unless the state or country in which enforcement of a judgment is sought has the defendant within its territorial reach, a foreign civil judgment remains merely an official paper. In short, jurisdiction to prescribe laws is not always hand-in-glove with jurisdiction to enforce them.

Under Indian law, in breach of contract cases, the cause of action arises in any of the following places[51]:

- Where the contract is made.
- Where the contract is to be performed, or the performance thereof is completed.
- Where, in performance of the contract, any money to which the suit relates is payable. or
- Where breach occurs.

Indian courts generally follow the same policies as English courts in connection with recognition and enforcement of foreign forum selection clauses in international commercial contracts.

European companies outsourcing to India should be aware, that inclusion of forum selection clauses within the agreements, which allocate jurisdiction to European courts, may still end up litigating in India, if an Indian court decides that the interests of justice will be better served by trial in India. The courts of India will not question the conclusiveness of a foreign judgment, and, thus its binding character, unless it can be established that the case falls within one of the six exceptions to CPC[52]. Parties cannot by agreement confer jurisdiction on a court which does not have jurisdiction under the CPC[53].

---

50 The concept of state sovereignty is a basic principle within international law, and means that a state has the power and the right to do what it wants within the confines laid down by international law; Shearer, I. A., Starkes International law (London Butterworth, 1994), p184.

51 Code of Civil Procedure, 1908 ("CPC"), s(20).

52 Ibid.

53 Ibid.

Where two or more Indian courts have jurisdiction under the CPC[54] to try a particular suit, an agreement between the parties that any dispute between them will be tried in one of such courts is binding[55].

While the intention of parties is usually given primacy, it is not dispositive[56]. In interpreting forum selection clauses, the following principles are applicable:

- The agreement must be clear and unambiguous.
- A unilateral declaration is ineffectual.
- It must appear that the party sought to be bound by the agreement had knowledge of the restrictive clause.
- The court may disregard the agreement if there are countervailing oppressive circumstances[57].
- The court mentioned in the agreement must be one which has jurisdiction to try the suit.
- A bare statement of jurisdiction of a court in the agreement is not enough; there should be an express exclusion of the jurisdiction of all other courts.

It is important that companies understand that clauses addressing certain issues cannot be governed by any other selected law[58]. These issues include those relating to (but not limited to):

- IP registration, protection and transfer.
- Real estate.
- Labour laws.
- Bankruptcy.

6.6.1 Nature and scope of section 13 of the Code of Civil Procedures, 1908

A foreign judgment may operate as res judicata[59] except in the six cases specified in section 13 and subject to other conditions in Section 11 of CPC[60]. The rules laid

---

54 Ibid.

55 Globe Transport Corporation v Triveni Engineering Works, (1983) 4 SCC 707; Hakam Singh v Gammon India Ltd., AIR 1971 SC 740; CIDC of Maharashtra v R. M. Mohite, 1998(3) Mh.L.J. 223; Ghatge & Patil v Madhusudan, AIR 1977 Bom 299. The plain meaning of "dispositive" is: "Being a deciding factor; bringing about a final determination." Black's Law Dictionary 484 (7th ed. 1999).

56 Having an effect on disposition or settlement.

57 All Bengal Transport Agency v Hare Krishna Bank AIR 1985 Gau 7.

58 i.e. they have to be governed by Indian Law because they are based on statutes of the country and contracts cannot exclude the law derived from statutes; Code of Civil Procedures, 1908.

down in this section are rules of substantive law and not merely of procedure. The six cases are:

1. Where it has not been pronounced by court of competent jurisdiction.
2. Where it has not been given on the merits of the case.
3. Where it appears on the face of the proceeding to be founded on an incorrect view of international law or a refusal to recognise the law of India in cases in which such law is applicable.
4. Where the proceeding in which the judgment was obtained is found to be opposed to natural justice.
5. Where it has been obtained by fraud.
6. Where it sustains a claim founded on a breach of any law in force in India.

Under section 44A of the CPC[61], a decree of any of the Superior Courts of any reciprocating territory[62] is executable as a decree passed by the domestic Court. Therefore in case the decree does not pertain to a reciprocating territory or a superior Court of a reciprocating territory, as notified by the Central Government in the Official Gazette, the decree is not directly executable in India. In case the decree pertains to a country which is not a reciprocating territory, then a fresh suit will have to be filed in India on the basis of such a decree or judgment[63].

Reciprocating territories include: United Kingdom of Great Britain and Northern Ireland, with the following being recognised as superior courts: the House of Lords, Court of Appeals, High Court of England, the Court of Sessions in Scotland, the High court in Northern Ireland, the Court of Chancery of the County Panlatine of Lancaster and the Court of Chancery of the county Palantine or Durham[64].

59 Res judicate is used to represent a legal case / proceedings which has undergone legal process and a judicial order is already issued on the same matter.

60 Code of Civil Procedure, 1908.

61 Ibid.

62 Reciprocating territory means any country or territory outside India which the Central Government may, by notification in the official Gazette, declare to be a reciprocating territory for the purposes of section 44A; and "superior courts', with reference to any such territory, means such Courts as may be specified in the said notification. Decree with reference to a superior court means any decree or judgment of such Court under which a sum of money is payable, not being a sum payable in respect of taxes or other charges of a like nature or in respect of a fine or other penalty, but shall in no case include an arbitration award, even if such an award is enforceable as a decree or judgment.

63 Moloji Nar Singh Rao v Shankar Saran, AIR 1962 SC 1737 at p.1748 para 14. Also see I & G Investment Trust v. Raja of Khalikote, AIR 1952 Cal. 508 at 523 para 38.

64 AIR Manual 5th edition, volume 4, declared by Government of India on 1.3.53.

Judgments passed by courts in these reciprocating territories can be enforced directly by filling execution proceedings under the CPC[65]. These foreign judgments are thus treated as decrees of an Indian court.

However in both cases the decree has to pass the test of s13 CPC[66] which specifies certain exceptions under which the foreign judgment becomes inconclusive and is therefore not executable or enforceable in India.

When a foreign judgment is founded on a jurisdiction or on a ground not recognized by Indian law or International Law, it is a judgment which is in defiance of the law. Hence, it is not conclusive of the matter adjudicated and, therefore, unenforceable in India, but the mistake must be apparent on the face of the proceedings.

6.7 Arbitration

The Law Commission of India has characterized the present judicial system as "stratified, highly expensive, inaccessible, unduly formal, lengthy and dilatory". The Law Commission and the Supreme Court have also suggested for such delays, that new dispute resolving machinery such as the Lok Adalats and Tribunals be set up.

The most commonly used forms of alternative dispute resolution include:

- Negotiation.
- Conciliation.
- Mediation.
- Arbitration.
- Settlement conference.
- Lok Adalat.

Arbitration the most frequently used alternative form of dispute resolution, is an alternative to full scale courtroom litigation. The benefit of putting an arbitration clause in a contract is that it is a confidential process with a binding result.

Arbitration is a process of dispute resolution in which a neutral third party (called the arbitrator) renders a decision after a hearing at which both parties have an opportunity to be heard. It is the means by which parties to a dispute get the same settled through the intervention of a third person, but without having recourse to a court of law[67].

---

65 Code Civil Procedure, 1908.

66 Ibid.

67 Indian Council of Arbitration (http://www.ficci.com).

The Arbitration and Conciliation Act 1996, governs both domestic and international arbitration in India. The Act, which took effect in August 1996, repealed the following Acts:

- The Arbitration (Protocol and Convention Act) 1937.
- The Arbitration Act 1940.
- The Foreign Awards (Recognition and Enforcement) Act 1961.

The Government has followed the United Nations Commission on International Trade Law Model Law in an effort to bring uniformity. The Act considerably reduces the power of the courts to intervene, with arbitral awards becoming automatically executable. The Act allows the parties to an arbitration agreement to determine the procedural and appointment of arbitrators as well as the substantive Law to be followed and the arbitral venue.

When the parties have entered into an arbitration agreement, they cannot file a suit in a court of law in respect of any matter covered by the agreement. The court will normally not intervene except where so provided by the Act[68].

6.7.1 What is an arbitration agreement?

Arbitration agreement means an agreement by the parties to submit to arbitration all or certain disputes which have arisen or which may arise between them in respect of a defined legal relationship whether contractual or not.

The arbitration agreement may be in the form of an arbitration clause in a contract or in the form of a separate agreement[69].

The process of arbitration is not governed by a well established set of case law and rules like litigation, so waiting for a final award can often be lengthier than may be imagined. Moreover the award of an arbitrator is typically difficult to appeal successfully. Arbitrators sometimes make decisions that are unexpected, since the decisions are frequently based on compromise. Therefore if arbitration is provided in the contract, it should state that the arbitration is to be governed by the terms of the contract, and insert such other provisions as may be necessary to restrict the arbitrator using his/her own opinion.

India is a party to the New York Convention and the Geneva Convention. A foreign arbitral award can be enforced in India.

---

68 Arbitration and Conciliation Act, 1996 (India): the Act is based on the UNCITRAL Model Law.

69 Where, however, there was no contract at all between the parties or contract was void ab initio, the arbitration clause cannot be enforced (Arbitration and Conciliation Act 1996).

Under the New York Convention, there are at least two laws which determine whether a dispute is arbitrable:

- The law of the seat of the arbitration, because no state is obliged to refer to arbitration a dispute that under its law is not arbitrable: Article II(1).
- The law of the country (or countries) where enforcement is sought, because the enforcement court may refuse enforcement of a dispute that is not arbitrable under its own law: Article V(2)(a).

However, the law of the seat is of primary importance. If a dispute is not arbitrable under that law, it is almost certain that the award will be set aside (or annulled), and in principle not be capable of enforcement in other countries.

A dispute is "arbitrable" when it is "capable of settlement by arbitration" (New York Convention, Article II (1)).

An arbitration agreement/clause must be in writing. Although no formal document is prescribed, however, it must be clear from the document that the parties had agreed to the settlement of dispute through arbitration. Where the arbitration agreement or clause is contained in a document, the parties must sign the document. Besides, the arbitration agreement may be established by[70]:

- An exchange of letters, telex, telegram or other means of telecommunication; or
- An exchange of statements of claim and defence in which the agreement is alleged by one party and is not denied by the other.

The parties to a dispute are free to determine the number of arbitrators, provided that it is not an even number. Arbitration will be conducted by a sole arbitrator unless otherwise requested.

If the parties cannot agree on the appointment of a sole arbitrator, or if any party fails to appoint its arbitrator, or if two arbitrators fail to appoint the third arbitrator, any party can apply to the Chief Justice of the relevant High Court for the appointment of an arbitrator. Where international commercial arbitration is involved[71], the appointment is made by the Chief Justice of the Supreme Court of India in New Delhi.

Arbitral awards are final and binding on the parties and persons claiming under them[72]. An aggrieved party can apply to the District Court or the High Court hav-

---

70 New York Convention, 1958.

71 Part I of the Act, which deals with conduct of arbitration proceedings, applies to arbitrations held in India. "International commercial arbitration" is arbitration of commercial issues in which at least one party is foreign.

72 In Jayesh H. Pandya vs. Sukanya Holdings Pvt. Ltd. AIR 2003, Bombay 148 the Supreme Court decided that the ambit and scope of Section 8 of the Arbitration and Con-

ing jurisdiction for setting aside such an award. It is possible to appeal certain interim orders of an arbitral tribunal. Any appeals to the High Court have to be made within 90 days from the date of the decree (or order); appeals to other courts have to be made within 30 days. There is no possibility of a second appeal. However, it may be possible to appeal to the Supreme Court.

6.7.2 Enforcement of foreign arbitral awards

"Foreign award" has been defined to mean an award on differences between persons arising out of legal relationships, whether contractual or not and considered as commercial under the law in force in India, and made in pursuance of an agreement in writing for arbitration to be governed either by the New York Convention or by the Geneva Convention, in the territory of a notified foreign state[73].

Where a commercial dispute covered by an arbitration agreement to which either of the conventions applies, arises before a judicial authority in India, it can at the request of a party be referred to arbitration. A suit based on foreign judgement must be filed in Indian courts, which could be a time consuming process. On the other hand an arbitral award obtained in the UK is enforceable in India, since India is a signatory to the United Nations Convention on the Recognition and Enforcement of Foreign Arbitral Awards (New York, 10 June 1958), hence arbitration whose seat is chosen to be a European country could be a quicker process for resolving disputes, than court litigation.

Typically outsourcers often don't want the dispute resolved in India – many agreements agree in advance to submit the dispute to an international arbitration group. London, Brussels and Geneva are popular places for multinational arbitration.

ciliation Act 1996. The Act does not oust the jurisdiction of the Civil Court to decide disputes where the parties to the arbitration agreement fail to take appropriate steps as contemplated under Sections 8(1) and (2). The Supreme Court agreed that the Act contains no specific provision to the effect that where the subject matter of a lawsuit includes the subject matter of an arbitration agreement, the matter must be referred to arbitration. However the term "a matter" in Section 8 indicates that in such cases the entire subject matter of a lawsuit should be subject to the arbitration agreement. In addition, the court held that Section 89 of the civil Procedure Code cannot be employed to interpret Section 8, and that it applies in the absence of an agreement to refer a dispute to arbitration.

[73] Arbitration and Conciliation Act, 1996.

6.8 Public policy and refusal to enforce foreign judgments / awards

Indian courts may refuse to enforce a foreign judgment / award, if it is contrary to the public good in India. Public policy is a means for each state to refuse to give effect in its territory to foreign acts (such as foreign judgments or awards) that it finds repugnant to the basic principles of its own legal order.

6.8.1 How courts apply the public policy limitation in international arbitration[74]

A very narrow notion is where it encompasses nothing short of the "most basic notions of morality and justice"[75] and the "requirements of substantial justice"[76]. This includes notably, rules protecting fundamental human rights, or generally "rights which outweigh contractual freedom". Contract terms may be unenforceable if they violate a fundamental public policy that clearly overrides the policy favouring enforcement of private transactions as between the parties. The principle that courts may invalidate a term of a contract on public grounds is recognised at common law[77].

The term "public policy" was interpreted in Renusagar Power Co. v. General Electric Co[78] by the Supreme Court where dealing with Section 7(1) (b) (ii) of the Foreign Awards (Recognition and Enforcement) Act, 1961 relating to enforcement of a foreign award took the view that "public policy" consisted of (a) the fundamental policy of Indian law, (b) the interests of India, and (c) justice and morality.

It is thus important that when wording the contract the parties are realistic and have due regard for Indian statutes and public policy even where the contract is based on European Law.

---

74 In ONGC v Saw Pipes Ltd the Supreme Court ruled that an award could be set aside if it is contrary to: fundamental domestic policy, domestic interests, justice or morality or domestic law. In Bharti International v Bulk Trading [2002] 37 SCL 434, the supreme court ruled that domestic courts have jurisdiction in respect of international commercial arbitration matters that take place abroad. Part 1 s(9) of the Act applies to arbitration proceedings held outside India. Parties to such proceedings can approach Indian courts for interim measures.

75 Parsons & Whittemore Overseas Co., Inc. v. Societe Generale de L'Industrie Du Papier (RAKTA). 508 F.2d 969; Europcar Italia, S.p.A. v. Maiellano Tours, Inc., 156 F.3d 310 (2d Cir. 1998). Inc (2nd Cir, 1999).

76 Minmetals v Ferco (High Court, England) [1999] 1 ALL ER (Comm) 315

77 Beverly Overseas SA v Privredna Bank Zagreb, 28 March 2001 (Swiss federal Supreme Court): award enforcing arms sale contract upheld).

78 Renusagar Power Co. v. General Electric Co 1994 Supp (1) SCC 644.

6.8.2 Application of Indian law in English courts[79]

Should there be some reason for a party to insist that Indian law should be applicable to a part of the contract, then factors that an English court will take into account need to be considered when dealing with a foreign law.

Broadly there are three different schemes in England to give effect to foreign judgments:

- Effect is given most readily to judgments from other parts of the United Kingdom, other Member States of the European Union under the Brussels I Regulation or states party to the Brussels or Lugano Convention . Here legislation has been implemented to provide rules that are easy to satisfy and provide a swift procedure for enforcement.
- Judgments from states party to bilateral agreements with the United Kingdom are dealt with under the statutory provisions that reflect the recognition and enforcement under common law, but benefit from a simplified enforcement procedure.
- Judgments from other countries are given effect according to the rules and the procedure at common law alone.

The Civil Jurisdiction and Judgments Act 1982 provide the mechanism for the recognition and enforcement of judgments under the Brussels and Lugano Conventions and also within the UK for judgments from Scotland, Northern Ireland and Gibraltar.

In England, the position is that an action in violation of an agreement, submitted to a foreign jurisdiction is normally stayed. In a situation where the parties are amenable to an English court's jurisdiction, an English court will allow the English action to continue if it considers that the ends of justice will be better served by trial in England[80]. Typical factors that will be considered include:

[79] In Bhatia International v Bulk Trading [2002] 37 SCL 434 the Supreme Court ruled that domestic courts have jurisdiction in respect of international commercial arbitration matters that take place abroad. The court was required to interpret the applicability of Part 1 of the Indian Arbitration and Conciliation Act 1996 to international commercial arbitration in view of the fact that Part 2 (which deals with the enforcement of foreign awards) makes no provision for interim measures. The court held that the legislature did not intend for Part 1 not to apply to arbitration that takes place outside India. Accordingly, Part 1, Section 9 of the Act applies to arbitration proceedings held outside India. Parties to such proceedings may now approach the Indian courts for interim measures.

[80] The Athenee (1992) 11 L1.L. Rep 6 as quoted in Cheshire & North's Private International Law, Butterworths, London 1987.

1. In which country is the evidence located?
2. Will the law of the foreign court apply, and if so, whether it differs from English law in any material respect?
3. With which country is either party connected and how closely?
4. Whether the defendant genuinely desires trial in the foreign country or is only seeking procedural advantages?
5. Whether the plaintiff will be prejudiced in having to sue in the foreign court?

There are four questions to be answered in the affirmative by an English judge before he can apply foreign law[81]:

1. In principle, following the rules of English law relating to choice of law, he must be convinced that foreign law is applicable to the issue – usually by expert evidence, orally or by affidavit[82].
2. English legislation must not prohibit the application of foreign law.
3. Foreign law must be pleaded and its applicability must be established by the party wanting to rely on it.
4. That party needs to prove the foreign law as a matter of fact to the satisfaction of the judge.

In order to hear and determine a case, the court seized needs to have been granted by law the power to do so, for which it needs to have jurisdiction. Jurisdiction is composed of personal and subject matter jurisdiction, both of which must be conferred on the court in question. English courts do not have jurisdiction for the following[83] (but not limited to):

- Claims involving the determination of a question of title to foreign land.
- Foreign patents or copyright issues, particularly validity.

Thus these two issues and others which are governed by Indian statute may not be conferred to any other Law than Indian Law.

In England the enforcement for foreign judgments is started by an application to the High Court, according to Arts 38 (2), 39 (1) and Annexe II to the Regulation, for an order to register the judgment for enforcement under Council Regulation (EC) 44/2001, complying with the formal requirements set out in Arts 53, 54 and Annexe V to the Regulation. Once the judgment is registered in this way it has the same force and effect and the court has the same powers as to its enforcement as if it were an English judgement.

---

81 A. Briggs, The conflict of laws, Oxford University Press, Clarendon Law Series, Oxford, 2002, pg 3-8.
82 S4 Civil Evidence Act 1972.
83 Pearce v Ove Arup Partnership Ltd (2000) Ch 403 (CA) and Briggs pg 48-51.

The next chapter examines some of the practical contractual considerations within an outsourcing agreement, and how the risks that arise as part of the outsourcing process can be reasonably allocated.

7. Allocation of risk into the contract

There are numerous risks that are apparent in any business deal, however, outsourcing by its nature creates additional risks that need to be assessed and apportioned in the contract. This chapter discusses the terms of the contract, disclaimers, subcontract provisions, privity of contract and general issues of insurance and force majeure.

7.1 Types of risks and terms within a contract

As in any contract agreement[84], specification of the scope of services and the allocation of responsibilities between the client and service provider is essential[85].

An important function of the outsourcing agreement is the allocation between the parties of the various risks associated with the contemplated transaction. The risk allocation schema poises one of the most difficult of issues between the customer and service provider.

There are numerous risks that are apparent in any business deal, however, outsourcing by its nature creates additional risks that need to be assessed and apportioned in the contract.

There are several risk categories that need to be considered as part of the agreement and relationship. These include (but are not limited to)[86]:

- Operational risk – such as poor service, or incomplete transactions[87] that disrupt operations and involve substantial direct and indirect losses.

---

84 Treitel defines a contract as: "an agreement giving rise to obligations which are enforced or recognised by law. The factor which distinguishes contractual from other legal obligations is that they are based on the agreement of the contracting parties." G.H. Treitel, the Law of Contract, 10th Edition, Sweet & Maxwell, London, 1999.

85 Outsourcing of all types of products and services has occurred for over a 100 years, however recent political interest in the potential for the loss of jobs to other countries and concerns of security and data protection have heightened concerns.

86 Allocating risks in Outsourcing, by George Kimball.

87 For instance where an outsourcing service provider is required to process payments made by the customers of the outsourcer, but due to computer system failure it fails to

- Financial risk – including excessive consumption of resources[88], project overruns, unexpected change requests[89] or third party charges.
- Scope – typically the most frequent source of friction after signing the contract.
- Security risk – such as disclosure of sensitive information to competitors through transfers of personnel, breaches of security or wrongdoing.
- Legal and Regulatory risks – affect not only such regulated industries as health care and banking, but increasingly most other businesses.
- Extraordinary risks – including the familiar circumstances that constitute force majeure. Parties must also consider other extraordinary risks and events, including acquisitions and divestitures, changes in control etc.

It is important to establish first that the law of contract forms part of the civil law, and is usually classified as part of the law of obligations. It is a body of rules which concerns itself with rights and actions between the persons who have created the contract. Sometimes, a contract situation can also be governed by protective rules of the criminal law.

Often, contracts will be in some way involved with property. In each case where a contract exists, you can assert your right in relation to the property by virtue of the agreement you have made. This difference can be significant, because in the law of contract, when you seek to enforce a contract, your normal remedy will be damages for breach, and it is not usual to get an order enforcing performance of the contract. If, on the other hand, you assert your rights under the law of property, the actual property is more likely to be restored to you.

Many Indian IT and call centre companies establish UK companies for the purpose of entering into contractual relations. However, such companies may in essence be "shell" companies with minimal assets, as they operate more as business development or marketing offices for the offshore operations. Customers must ensure that if a service provider is unlikely to have sufficient assets to meet any claims under the respective contract, that there is at least an obligation on the service provider to maintain an appropriate insurance policy in place to meet any potential claims. If a European service provider office has neither sufficient assets nor insurance, then consideration should be given to either contracting directly with a parent Indian company which is more financially sound or alternatively obtaining a parent company guarantee.

---

do so in the time stipulated. This may have further consequences which impact upon the outsourcers business, such as cash flow problems, damage to reputation etc.

88 For instance an agreed activity may take much longer to complete that may have been estimated.

89 Where the outsource service provider may request some contract activity terms to be changed after due experience, that may not have been anticipated and which may render the original financial business case to be such that it creates serious financial risk.

India has a written contract Act[90] and all agreements are subject to this statute and thus agreements must be carefully drafted in accordance with Indian law[91]. One of the main issues that arise is the issue of enforcing non-compete provisions. India has stringent laws against restrictive trade practices and thus enforceability of stand alone non-compete provisions on termination of a contract are questionable[92].

The main demands for contract consideration should include:

- Limitation of Liability - Outsourcing agreements often contain a cap on direct damages for which a party may be liable. This cap can be an absolute amount or a percentage of the fees paid or to be paid under the agreement. Liquidated damages at its simplest takes the assessment of damages out of the courts and replaces them with a simpler matrix of fixed costs for non-performance. The most common form of liquidated damages in an outsourcing contract is service credits. Liquidated damages are intended to be focusing, not punitive and to be enforceable, should represent a reasonable pre-estimate of the likely direct loss of the claiming party. As such, an overriding limit is normally placed in the total value of liquidated damages over a specified period.
- Exclusion of Consequential Damages - Most outsourcing agreements will (or will at least attempt to) contain an exclusion of any special, indirect, exemplary, incidental or consequential damages (including loss of profits).
- Indemnification - The indemnification clause identify claims and causes of actions from which each party will protect the other (e.g. the service provider may indemnify the customer from any damages arising from claims made by the service provider's employees).
- Disclaimers - The agreement will also likely disclaim other warranties and set forth certain situations for which a party will not be held responsible (e.g., malfunctions of third-party software).

---

90 The Indian Contract Act of 1872, which defines the legal framework for writing and honouring contracts, including breach of contracts and Indemnity of contracts.

91 Where the proper law is determined to be UK law, there may still be a requirement to satisfy Indian law specifically in areas which are deemed to be in the public good.

92 Article 81 of the Treaty of Rome also imposes restrictions with regard to contracts in restraint of trade, where such contracts hinder trade between member states. Article 85 concerns agreements which have as their object or effect the prevention, restriction or distortion of competition within the common market. Significantly, Article 81 is of "direct effect". This means that it creates rights for individuals which can be enforced and protected by direct legal action in the English courts. Investigation by the European Commission can also result in fines. If such an agreement is found to violate Article 81, it is void. Under Article 81(3) it is possible for the European Commission to grant exemption from these rules. Unless an exemption has been granted, the agreement breaching Article 81 is unenforceable.

7.2 Terms of a contract

Outsourcing agreements should distinguish between representations, warranties and covenants[93].

Traditionally, terms have been divided into two categories, conditions and warranties. A condition is a major term which is vital to the main purpose of the contract. A breach of condition will entitle the injured party to repudiate the contract and claim damages. The injured party may also choose to go on with the contract, despite the breach, and recover damages instead[94]. A warranty is a less important term - it does not go to the root of the contract. A breach of warranty will only give the injured party the right to claim damages; the party cannot repudiate the contract[95].

The Sale of Goods Act 1979 within the UK, for instance, defines a condition as a term (in a contract of sale) that would, if broken, entitle the other party to repudiate the contract, whereas breach of a warranty could lead only to damages.

The difficult question faced by lawyers is how to distinguish between the conditions and warranties. As a general proposition, the weight of a term depends on the intention of the parties. Although intention is important, it must be looked at objectively. The mere fact that the parties have used the words "condition" or "warranty" does not necessarily mean that they have correctly classified the term.

Customers often have sufficient leverage to insist that various commitments be phrased as representations or warranties. For their part, customers resist warranting the condition of among other things their assets and facilities.

It was always thought that the classification of the terms was established at the point when the contract was made. However, in some cases, it was clear that such early classification could produce unfair results.

In cases where the courts were not bound by a classification imposed by statute or existing precedents, the judges began to explore the effect of leaving the classification until they saw the outcome of the breach. In these cases, the court considers the term to be innominate or intermediate, and only classifies once the seriousness of the breach and resulting harm is known. The creation of such third category so-called “innominate terms”, in which the remedy depends on the seriousness of the actual consequences, complicates matters further.

---

93 A covenant is an agreement between two or more persons, entered into in writing and under seal, whereby either party stipulates for the truth of certain facts, or promises to perform or give something to the other, or to abstain from the performance of certain things.

94 Poussard v Spiers (1876) 1 QBD 410.

95 Bettini v Gye (1876) 1 QBD 183.

Where the outsourcing contract states the governing law for the contract to be that of a particular country (e.g. the UK), then the terms of the contract need to be carefully drafted to ensure conformance with applicable laws of that country, including statutes and case law (e.g. UK laws and case history).

7.2.1 Defining terms

It was established in Heilbut, Symons & Co v Buckleton[96], that intention is the overall guide as to whether a statement is a term of the contract. In seeking to implement the parties' intentions and decide whether a statement is a term or a mere representation, the courts will consider the following four factors:

1. Timing - The court will consider the lapse of time between the making of the statement and the contract's conclusion: if the interval is short the statement is more likely to be a term[97].
2. Importance of the statement - The court will consider the importance of the truth of the statement as a pivotal factor in finalising the contract[98].
3. Reduction of terms to writing - The court will consider whether the statement was omitted in a later, formal contract in writing. If the written contract does not incorporate the statement, this would suggest that the parties did not intend the statement to be a contractual term.
4. Special knowledge/skills - The court will consider whether the maker of the statement had specialist knowledge or was in a better position than the other party to verify the statement's accuracy[99].

Many outsourcing contracts contain customary representations and warranties concerning corporate power and authority, good standing and the absence of defaults, or conflicts with any law. These are rarely controversial, although some may be limited to material issues.

7.2.2 Intermediate terms

It may be impossible to classify a term neatly in advance as either a condition or a warranty. Some undertakings may occupy an intermediate position, in that the term can be assessed only in the light of the consequences of a breach. If a breach of the term results in severe loss and damage, the injured party will be entitled to repudiate the contract; where the breach involves minor loss, the injured party's

96 Heilbut, Symons & Co v Buckleton [1913] AC 30.
97 Routledge v McKay [1954] 1 WLR 615.
98 Couchman v Hill [1947] 1 All ER 103.
99 Dick Bentley Productions v Harold Smith Motors [1965] 2 All ER 65.

remedies will be restricted to damages[100]. These intermediate terms have also become known as innominate terms.

7.2.3 Implied terms

In most contracts the primary obligations of the parties are contained in express terms. In addition there are various circumstances in which extra terms may be implied into the agreement.

7.2.3.1 Terms implied by custom

The terms of a contract may have been negotiated against the background of the customs of a particular locality or trade[101] – this is relevant in the context of outsourcing to an India based service provider - e.g. SLA metrics may be more loosely defined, or the service provider may consider most terms within the contract to be warranties and not conditions.

7.2.3.2 Terms implied by the court

The courts may be prepared to imply a term into a contract in order to give effect to the obvious intentions of the parties[102], although this is usually rare.

7.2.3.3 Terms implied by statute

Both parties usually covenant to comply with applicable laws and regulations[103], and represent that (at least as disclosed) no proceedings are pending or threatened concerning alleged violations. When employees are transferred, or the service provider operates from customer facilities, particular attention should be paid to health, safety, environmental and employment laws. When assets are transferred, service providers may request additional, specific protections, as in any other purchase of assets.

Where assets change hands and employees are transferred, the representations and warranties resemble those seen in business acquisitions. Occasionally, one side or the other may request representations to the effect that customer disclosures or service provider proposals are complete, accurate and without material omissions.

---

[100] Hong Kong Fir Shipping Co v Kawasaki Kisen Kaisha [1962] 1 All ER 474; Bunge Corporation v Tradax Export [1981] 2 All ER 513.

[101] Hutton v Warren (1836) 150 ER 517.

[102] Liverpool City Council v Irwin [1976] 2 All ER 39.

[103] Such as the: The Sale of Goods Act 1979; The Supply of Goods and Services Act 1982; and The Sale and Supply of Goods Act 1994.

It should be noted that customer data and disclosures are rarely complete and service provider do not generally warrant sales presentations.

7.2.4 Typical service provider requests[104]

The service provider may ask for numerous representations and warranties, the most common include:

- Clear title to transferred assets, free from liens and security interests – consideration must be given to any existing security interest which may be covered by a floating charge[105] over all equipment.
- Customers usually transfer assets to the service provider at commencement of the agreement, and thus service providers usually require representations that the transferred equipment is in good working condition, excluding wear and tear. In practice the customer usually warrants that the equipment has been maintained to the manufacturer's specification.
- That the service provider has received all licenses and lease agreement and that there are no material uncured defaults under leases, maintenance contracts, software licenses and other third party contracts assigned to the service provider.
- Customer operational and consumption and similar data used to determine charges for the customer by the service provider are accurate. Typically customers refuse to do so and thus the service provider's prices are usually subject to adjustment clauses.
- Hardware, software and other assets transferred or made available to perform services are sufficient for that purpose.
- There are no violations of law, or pending or threatened proceedings concerning transferred assets, contract and employees.

7.2.5 Typical customer requests

In a similar manner to service provider requests, customers may seek representations and warranties to protect its interests. These may include:

- Covenant or warranties to the effect that the service provider will deliver good professional service that meets or exceeds "good industry standards". The diffi-

---

[104] Adapted from Arnold Porter, Allocating risks in outsourcing.

[105] It is normal that a bank will in the normal course of events seek to take security for a loan by way of either fixed or floating charge. A floating charge hovers over the ever changing assets until a certain event happens which turns it into a fixed charge (crystallized). It is at that time, and not before, that the borrower is no longer able to deal freely with those assets to which the floating charge attaches.

culty however lies with the definition of "good industry standard" and usually involves some form of benchmarking.
- Covenants to maintain equipment and software, and keep them up-to-date through regular replacements. However, this may be difficult to obtain, as service providers usually require flexibility to choose its own maintenance schedules and as long as the service provider delivers the service, it should not be an issue for the customer.
- Covenants to perform efficiently and minimise charges. Most charges are consumption based and may depend in part upon efficiency. Customers usually want the service provider to guarantee efficiency levels so as to minimise costs.
- Covenants or warranties concerning detection and eradication of viruses. Since most outsourced services are critical to the customer's business, potential viruses could inflict serious financial damages and protection against such risks is important.
- Warranties concerning the quality of hardware and software products supplied under the outsourcing contract. This becomes especially important when the agreement is terminated and the customer may wish to bring the service back in-house.

And typically in offshore contracts:

- Representations and warranties that the service provider has not offered any improper inducements to win the business, especially where such practice may be inherent in the country – something that may be relevant in the case of India.

For long term contracts, the service provider should assume certain predictable risks of technology changes. Beyond a certain point, such as three to five years, changes in technology are speculative. Both sides must provide contractual leeway to benefit from such changes without incurring material adverse consequences if those changes should radically alter the contractual balance. A set of procedures for "co-sourcing" or "joint sourcing" of decisions can facilitate effective communications, planning and implementation of changes.

7.3 Disclaimers

Customers inevitably will need to accept that disclaimers will be part of the contract but must ensure that a disclaimer does not void the warranty and indemnity provisions.

Service providers typically propose to disclaim the following, but which the customer may wish to avoid:

- Warranties concerning the accuracy of any advice, reports or data delivered to the customer, or business results from action the customer may take based on the service provider's advice, reports or data.
- Any warranty or assurance that any service or the operation of any computer, network or other system will be uninterrupted or error-free. Service providers reason that technology is imperfect, and even the most stringent service levels leave some slight margin for error – however, such issues must be included as part of a well defined and drafted Service Level Agreement (SLA) – not a blanket disclosure.

7.4 Subcontracting provisions

It is likely that the outsourcing service provider will not be able to perform all its tasks by itself. Subcontracting of tasks, such as equipment and operating system software maintenance, is common because the service provider of those products are often more familiar with the products and more efficient in maintaining them. The outsourcing agreement should require that the service provider be responsible and liable for the acts and omissions of any and all subcontractors.

If the level of responsibility or risks created by the subcontractor are high the customer may also wish to be included as a third party beneficiary which can enforce the terms of the subcontractors if the prime contractor fails to do so.

7.5 Privity of contract

"The doctrine of privity means that a contract cannot, as a general rule, confer rights or impose obligations arising under it on any person except the parties to it[106]."

However, there are many exceptions to the doctrine that have been developed, which attempt to preserve justice: e.g. Agency[107], trusts[108] and restrictive covenants[109].

The House of Lords affirmed in 1980, the view that a contracting party cannot recover damages for the loss sustained by the third party[110].

---

106 GH Treitel, The Law of Contract.

107 Scruttons Ltd v Midland Silicones Ltd [1962] AC 446.

108 Les Affreteurs Reunis v Leopold Walford [1919] AC 801.

109 Tulk v Moxhay (1848) 2 Ph 774.

110 Woodar Investment Development v Wimpey Construction [1980] 1 WLR 277.

However, within the UK, since the coming into force of the Contracts (Rights of Third Parties) Act 1999 which abolished the doctrine of privity of contract and allowed certain third parties (either specifically identified people or members of a particular class, on whom a contract expressly confers a benefit, or purports to confer a benefit) to enforce a term of the contract, it is advisable to note the interest of certain third parties in particular clauses of the agreement.

The third parties rights are subjected to the same defences as the parties have against one another, but otherwise are additional to, and not in substitution for existing third party rights.

India does not expressly recognise the concept of "third party beneficiary" which entitles a third party to sue for enforcement of a contract made for its benefit, although certain enforcement rights can be created as a matter of general contract law if the third party and the obligated contracting party sign a written document that expressly acknowledges the third party's enforcement rights[111].

A contract between two parties may be accompanied by a collateral contract between one of them and a third person relating to the same subject matter. There must however be evidence of an intention to create a collateral contract before that contract can be formed.

7.6 Insurance requirements

The outsourcing service provider should be required to as part of the agreement, to obtain adequate insurance to provide financial protection for the indemnifications it provides to the customer. This may include: professional liability insurance to protect against the service provider's negligence; liability insurance for injuries and death; and worker's compensation insurance.

7.7 Force Majeure provisions

Agreements typically include a provision that neither party has liability for delays or failures that are caused by events outside the reasonable control of the party, including the acts or omissions of the other party.

A typical force majeure provision looks something like the following:

[111] Indian Contract Act and Geetanjali Woolen Private Ltd v M. V X-Press Annapurna and Others (Bombay High Court) (09/08/2005).

- Neither party shall be liable for any delay in, or failure of, its performance of any of its obligations under this Agreement if such delay or failure is caused by events beyond the reasonable control of the affected party, including but not limited to any acts of God, government embargoes, restrictions, quarantines, strikes, riots, wars or other military action, civil disorder, acts of terrorism, rebellions or revolutions, fires, floods, vandalism, sabotage or acts of third parties.

All too often, many outsourcing agreements (actually virtually all contracts) tend to insert a standard force majeure provision without giving it a second thought (seen as something that is not likely to happen and therefore does not warrant too much time and attention). However, in many respects a force majeure provisions has the potential to have serious implications for the enforcement of a contract. A too widely drafted provision can undo all the hard work gone into drafting terms for contract enforcement.

It is more useful to break a force majeure provision down and examine the cause of force majeure events, such as:

- Those physical events that are foreseeable, although unpredictable, such as fire, floods or vandalism.
- Those day-to-day business events or government actions that cannot be forecast, but which are foreseeable, such as strikes or regulatory activities.
- Those events although still rare are possible such as military action, embargoes, rebellions and terrorism.
- Those events caused by extraordinary elements of nature or acts of God which are truly unforeseeable force majeure events.

As a customer of an outsourced service, you cannot afford to lose service no matter what the cause of the problem.

Increasingly lawyers are reclassifying force majeure events into three categories:

1. Relatively common events related to either business or governmental acts or other foreseeable accidents or acts of nature.
2. Uncommon events not within the parties control, but for which the parties must assume the risk of occurrence.
3. Truly unforeseeable events caused by extraordinary elements of nature or acts of God.

Parties are increasingly not relieving the non-performing party of any liability upon the occurrence of a force majeure event, but creating a particular set of obligations and actions the non-performing party must undertake, triggered by a particular event – i.e. a risk management approach to contract enforcement.

A force majeure provision should attempt to classify force majeure events into those that are truly unforeseeable and unpreventable and those that have some degree of control. It should furthermore attempt to bring into focus practical issues to ensure continuity of services through disaster recovery programs which the service provider should have implemented – clearly this will be a debating issue between parties and will depend on the criticality of the services provided by the service provider.

7.8 Disaster recovery

Most organisations that outsource services typically outsource an element which consists of IT. Such organisations are very dependent on their IT infrastructure to support their business processes and deliver competitive advantage. If a disaster affects their ability to operate the IT infrastructure, business processes stop, and they lose market share. It is thus important to plan for potential disasters and how services are continued to be made available.

Typically a customer will insist that the service provider plan and if necessary implement a Disaster Recovery Plan. A disaster can be defined as any event, which would inhibit the service provider, providing normal service. A disaster recovery plan could involve duplication of various IT systems at a secure remote location, and the requirements to back-up all data and transactions, which can be re-instated when a disaster recovery plan is enacted.

In reality, there may be more than one disaster recovery plan, each specifically addressing a particular aspect of the service or services.

Each Disaster Recovery Plan should incorporate at a minimum the existing processes and procedures and the infrastructure and personnel currently in place that the service provider will use in providing Disaster Recovery services, including information regarding disaster recovery planning and testing capabilities, disaster recovery invocation procedures, recovery site management and standard backup and recovery procedures. These plans should be updated and maintained by the service provider and be modified to reflect changes in Disaster Recovery requirements.

The Disaster Recovery Plans should be maintained and updated by the service provider so that they continue to reflect the contemporaneous state of the services being provided to the service provider.

7.8.1 Disaster recovery testing

The service provider should carry out regular testing of the Disaster Recovery Services at the frequencies set out as appropriate and in accordance the Disaster Recovery Plans.

7.8.1.1 Provision of disaster recovery services

On the declaration of a disaster by either of the parties, the service provider should:

- Take all such steps as are stipulated by the Disaster Recovery Plan in order to restore the supply of all services directly affected by the disaster.
- Achieve the recovery of the services in accordance with and within the recovery time-scale requirements set out in the existing services recovery service levels.
- Take such further steps as may reasonably be expected from the service provider as a leading supplier of such services and/or such steps as are at its disposal.
- Ensure that during the recovery period the services are provided in accordance with the Disaster Recovery Plan.
- Use all reasonable endeavours to ensure that all services indirectly affected by the disaster continue to be provided in accordance with the service levels during the recovery period.
- Ensure that all services which are not directly or indirectly affected by the disaster continue to be provided in accordance with the service levels.

The next chapter discusses how good project management can reduce some of the risks within outsourcing, and includes issues good governance and performance / quality management.

8. Project management

This chapter discusses project management as a holistic process, which includes transition planning, good governance and performance / quality management. Outsourcing customers should require a preliminary transition plan before the contract is signed.

8.1 Elements of good project management

Project planning and management are critical disciplines to enable successful outsourcing initiatives - Gantt charts and critical path analysis, although important disciplines do not go far enough. Companies need to include the effective use of the people who possess the appropriate project management and risk management skills and experience with the ability to use the right tools and programs to get the work done.

Members of outsourcing teams need to also bring with them specific knowledge regarding the outsourced product or function, business and stakeholder objectives, and the knowledge of the market and the skills to analyse the potential supply market and associated risks for the product or service to be outsourced.

Team members must also be able to think critically about, and assess, what could go wrong and put sourcing and risk mitigation/contingency strategies and plans in place to handle those scenarios.

Offshore program and project management broadly involve three critical activities:

1. Transition Management.
2. Governance.
3. Performance and Quality Management.

8.1.1 Transition management

Smooth transition management is considered to be a critical success factor in outsourcing. Transition management includes the detailed, desk-level knowledge transfer and documentation of all relevant tasks, technologies, workflows, and functions (and in some cases employees). The transition period is the most complex stage of an outsourcing process lasting up to a year to complete.

Transition management involves the following:

- Developing transition plan (key activities, milestones, resources, dependencies).
- Facilitating transition operations and/or initiation of projects.
- Transferring knowledge of internal procedures and processes.
- Managing strategic and operational communications.
- Managing employees - redeploying, transfer, or terminate.
- Documenting lessons learned to improve service provider management.

8.1.2 Governance

Governance focuses on proactive and collaborative management of the relationship, the evolution of services provided, ongoing communication processes, performance review standards, and overall project management, and goes beyond simply monitoring of contractual obligations.

Ongoing governance involves the following:

- Project management - communication, collaboration, and monitoring of the service provider.
- Relationship management - necessary to compensate for the loss of direct interaction between stakeholders, managers, and team members.
- Change management - ensures that standardized procedures are used for efficient, prompt handling of all changes.
- Risk management - describes the processes concerned with identifying, analysing, and responding to outsourcing partnership risks.

8.1.3 Performance and quality management

With organizations outsourcing almost every aspect of their operations, multiple service providers participating in sourcing deals, business users and governance teams residing in separate locations, challenges to coordinate interactions, manage performance, monitor contract terms and track financial metrics, a disciplined, continuous improvement program is a necessity for long-term success.

Ongoing governance involves the following:

- Continuous performance reporting - measures outsourcing effectiveness using appropriate metrics, SLAs, and business case.
- Quickly implementing improvements and adjustments.
- Evaluating feasibility of additional outsourcing.

The next chapter discusses the various methods available to reduce liability within contract and the importance of statutory legislation which may limit the extent to which certain liabilities can be excluded.

9. Contract discharge and methods to reduce liability

This chapter discusses possible interpretations of contract discharge and the various methods available to reduce liability. It details issues in relation to: consequential losses, limits on damages that may be awarded, indemnities and the application of the Unfair Contract Terms legislation in clauses attempting to reduce liability.

9.1 Contract performance

Clauses may seek to exclude or limit liability which would otherwise arise in the event of a breach of contract. If they are drafted appropriately, these clauses can be valid. The principle of freedom of contract still operates, but it is recognised that there is great scope for abuse of exemption and limitation clauses, particularly where the parties are not of equal bargaining strength, or where they are using standard form contracts.

A contract can be discharged by agreement, performance, breach (including anticipatory breach) or frustration. It is important to understand what is meant by discharge, as the effect of these methods of discharge can be different:

- Discharge by agreement - Generally, the parties can agree to discharge an existing contract, and their agreement will be legally binding, provided it satisfies the normal contract principles. The difficulty is usually in finding a valid consideration to support the agreement to discharge. This is not a problem where neither party has performed, as each promises to forego the performance of the other.
- Discharge by performance - Generally, the parties must exactly and precisely perform the obligations they have taken on under the contract. If they both do so, the contract is discharged by their performance. If one party fails in any way, he will be in breach of contract. The scale of the breach depends on whether he has broken a major or minor term of the contract. Minor breaches (breach of warranty) only give rise to a right to sue for damages. If a party exercises the right to repudiate the contract, then the contract can be said to be discharged. As a general rule, a person who only partially performs (and the injured is not happy to accept partial performance, or if the party has been pre-

vented from fully discharging its obligations) is not entitled to be paid[112], unless the courts find the contract to be divisible.

- Discharge by breach – Only when there is a breach of a major term will the injured party have the right to treat the contract as discharged. If this right is available to an injured party, he may elect to affirm the contract. This means that he decides to go ahead with performance despite the breach. This keeps alive all the obligations of both parties[113]. If the injured party elects to treat the contract as discharged, this effectively discharges the parties from further performance. However, the contract has existed and has been valid up to that point. The effect of the injured party treating the contract as discharged affects the primary obligations under the contract. Secondary obligations, such as the obligation to pay damages for breach, are still in force.
- Anticipatory Breach - Sometimes, one party by his words or behaviour, makes clear that he is not going to perform his obligations under the contract. Where repudiation takes place before the date due for performance in the contract, it is called anticipatory breach. A victim of such a breach can wait for the due date of performance, and then sue for actual breach. Or, he may sue at once, treating the contract as discharged by the anticipatory breach. If one party believes that the other has committed an anticipatory breach, he may react by accepting the repudiation and treating it as discharging the contract. If it then transpires that the behaviour is not a repudiatory anticipatory breach, then the party treating the contract as discharged may now find that he in turn is regarded as being in breach[114].
- Discharge by frustration - In some cases, events may occur which make it impossible for one of the parties to carry out his part of the bargain. The contract principle used to be that any non-performance amounted to breach. This rule has now been diluted by the development of principles relating to frustration. These rules developed by the courts are only relevant if the parties have not provided themselves for the difficulties encountered[115]. Where there is no provision made by the parties, then the rules developed by the courts will have the effect of terminating the contract in appropriate cases, and the financial arrangements between the parties will then be dealt with under the Law Reform (Frustrated Contracts) Act 1943 in the UK for instance. The event relied on to frustrate the contract must be outside the control of both parties. If one of them has been able to exercise some kind of control or election, then there is no frustration[116]. Section 2(3) of the Frustrated Contracts Act provides that where the parties themselves have provided a solution within their contract, that solu-

112 Bolton v Mahadeva [1972] 2 All ER 1322 and Cutter v Powell [1795] at p 427 and 426.

113 Fercometal SARL v Mediterranean Shipping Co [1988] 2 All ER and Avery v Bowden [1855] 5 El & Bl 714.

114 Federal Commerce Ltd v Molena Appha Inc [1979] 1 All ER 307 and Woodar Investment Ltd v Wimpey UK Ltd [1980] 1 All ER 571.

115 Bangladesh Export Co v Sucden Kerry SA [1995] 2 Lloyds Rep 1.

116 Maritime National Fish Co v Ocean Trawlers [1935] AC 524 and Lauritzen v Wijsmuller BV [1990] 1 Lloyds Rep 1.

tion will be applied to the exclusion of the Act, subject to the "true construction of the contract".

9.2 Representations and warranties

Representations and warranties are often paired with corresponding indemnities. Often, the principal indemnities are reciprocal.

Outsourcing contracts invariably limit the service provider's liability (and often, both parties' liability) by:

- Precluding recovery of indirect, punitive and consequential damages.
- Imposing a ceiling upon recovery of actual damages, subject to
- Some narrow exceptions for infringements, wrongdoing and other remote, but serious risks.

A clause may be inserted into a contract which aims to exclude or limit one party's liability for breach of contract or negligence. However, the party may only rely on such a clause if it has been incorporated into the contract, and if as a matter of interpretation, it extends to the loss in question. Its validity will also need to be tested under the national laws which restrict unfair contract terms, such as the UK Unfair Contract Terms Act 1977.

The person wishing to rely on the exclusion clause must show that it formed part of the contract[117]. An exclusion clause can be incorporated in the contract by signature, by notice, or by a course of dealing. The clause must be contained in a contractual document, i.e. one which a reasonable person would assume to contain contractual terms, with sufficient notice been given of the exclusion clause[118].

9.2.1 Consequential damages

Outsourcing contracts uniformly restrict, and often prohibit, recovery of lost profits or other consequential damages. Customers with sufficient bargaining leverage sometimes secure limited rights to recover consequential damages, up to a negotiated ceiling, in situations where the only damages are virtually certain to be consequential, such as misappropriations of confidential information and intellectual property. Contracts more frequently permit recovery (as indemnified losses) of consequential damages paid to third parties and classify various costs related to corrective action as direct, rather than indirect or consequential damages.

---

[117] Unfair Contract Terms Act, 1977, s7(3) and s(11).

[118] Contra Proferentem rule: Ailsa Craig Fishing Co Ltd v Malvern Fishing Company [1983] 1 All ER 101 (HL).

9.2.2 Limits on recovery of actual damages

Ceilings upon actual damages are sometimes fixed sums (as in an insurance policy). More often, ceilings equal the total charges during an agreed number of months.

Customers as would be expected prefer higher limits. For the customer (and, in practice, both sides) the questions are similar to those surrounding limits upon insurance coverage.

Liability limits are sometimes the last major issue to be decided, and outcomes vary, depending upon the scale of the transaction, the parties' bargaining leverage, the presence or absence of competition, the number and extent of exceptions, and resolution of other major issues.

For the very worst contingencies, such as intentional wrongdoing, liability may be unlimited. The existence of limits upon recovery makes other remedies – notably termination – all the more important to the customer.

9.3 Indemnities

There are numerous indemnities that parties to the contract will attempt to incorporate within the agreement. Some of these will be those the customer seeks from the service provider, some will be when the service provider seek indemnity from the customer. In addition some indemnities will be reciprocal, when parties will be seeking each other to indemnify against common material issues.

9.3.1 Mutual indemnities

Many indemnities are mutual and symmetrical. Each side, for example, usually indemnifies the other against personal injury and property damage claims. These kinds of claims are often insured, and not usually controversial. Typical mutual or reciprocal indemnities include:

- Claims by transferred employees concerning their employment. The customer is generally responsible for claims arising before transfer. Thereafter, the service provider bears responsibility. The service provider should also be responsible for acts or omissions in its selection of transferred employees before the contract was signed.
- Claims concerning equipment leases, software licenses, maintenance agreements and other contracts transferred to the service provider. Again, the customer is responsible before transfer, and the service provider, thereafter.
- Breaches of confidentiality.

- Infringement of patents, copyrights, trade secrets and other intellectual property rights. The indemnitor generally insists upon reasonable flexibility to defend claims. Customers want assurance of continuous service however the service provider may deal with any claims of infringement.
- Violations of law. Each side generally indemnifies the other against claims concerning its violations of applicable law.

9.3.2 Service provider indemnities

Customers sometimes request additional indemnities from their service provider:

- Apart from the basic obligation to comply with laws, and indemnify the customer against violations, service providers are sometimes asked to defend the customer against failures to comply with legal or regulatory requirements attributable to the service provider's acts or omissions.
- Customers sometimes propose that service provider indemnify them against claims covered by whatever insurance the contract may require.
- Where services are provided from facilities shared with other customers, a customer may require indemnification against any claims arising from shared use.

9.3.3 Customer indemnities

When service providers buy assets, and especially facilities, they may seek (as noted earlier) representations and warranties concerning title to those assets, the assets' condition, and the facilities' compliance with health, safety and environmental laws. They may also request corresponding indemnities, or a blanket indemnity against all claims related to their representations and warranties.

Indemnity provision should be considered for the following:

- Intellectual Property - In cases where the service provider infringes copyright, patents or trademarks or misappropriated trade secrets. Protection of buyer from 3rd party claims and actions for IP that may have been gained wrongfully.
- Injuries to persons or property caused by the service provider.
- Negligence and wilful misconduct.
- Compliance with laws and regulations.

9.4 Limiting liability

Liability may be limited by the use of exclusion clauses in the contract. If there is any ambiguity or uncertainty as to the meaning of an exclusion clause, the court will construe it contra proferentum, i.e. against the party who inserted it in the contract[119].

Under the main purpose rule, a court can strike out an exemption clause which is inconsistent with or repugnant to the main purpose of the contract[120].

9.5 European Unfair Contract Terms

In April 1993, the EC Directive on Unfair Contract Terms was adopted[121]. The directive aims to prohibit the use of unfair terms in consumer contracts which have not been individually negotiated. Its scope is stated in Article as being limited to contracts between a consumer and a seller or supplier. More recently, Directive 2005/29/EC[122] came into force in May 2005. The Unfair Commercial Practices Directive is intended to combine a high level of consumer protection with the removal of obstacles to cross-border trade within the European Union arising from differences in fair trading laws from country to country.

The Directive requires the member states to pass laws by no later than June 12, 2007 giving effect to it in national law by December 12, 2007. The Directive is concerned mainly with the standards of behaviour required of traders. To some extent it leaves to member states the choice of appropriate domestic enforcement procedures and penalties for non-compliance. There is a general prohibition on unfair business-to-consumer commercial practices[123] (there application to outsourcing contracts is therefore minimal). "Unfair commercial practices" are in effect defined as practices which are "contrary to the requirements of professional diligence".

9.5.1 The UK Unfair Contract Terms Act (UCTA) 1977

The basic purpose of UCTA 1977 is to restrict the extent to which liability in a contract can be excluded for breach of contract and negligence, largely by refer-

119 Baldry v Marshall [1925] 1 KB 260.

120 Evans Ltd v Andrea Merzario Ltd [1976] 1 WLR 1078.

121 Directive 93/13 EEC, OJ 95, 21/4/93.

122 Official Journal of the European Union, L149/22 - L149/39, 11th June 2005.

123 Articles 3(1) and 5(1).

ence to a reasonableness requirement, but in some cases by a specific prohibition[124].

Most of the provisions of the Act apply only to what is termed "business liability". This is defined by s1(3) as liability arising from things done by a person in the course of a business or from the occupation of business premises.

9.5.2 Main provisions of UCTA 1977 relevant to outsourcing contracts

9.5.2.1 Exemption of liability for negligence

No one acting in the course of a business can exclude or restrict his liability in negligence for death or personal injury by means of a term in a contract or by way of notice[125]. It is possible to exclude liability for negligence for any other kind of loss or damage provided the term or notice satisfies the requirement of reasonableness[126].

9.5.2.2 Exemption of liability for breach of contract

Where one party deals on the other party's written standard terms of business, then the other party cannot exclude or restrict his liability for breach of contract, non-performance of the contract or different performance of the contract unless the exemption clause satisfies the requirement of reasonableness[127]. It is unlikely in an outsourcing contract that the customer will deal on the other party's standard terms of business - rather it will be quite unusual for the contract not to have been intensely negotiated.

9.5.2.3 Exemption of implied terms in contracts of sale

In contracts for the sale of goods, the implied terms as to title cannot be excluded or restricted by a contract term[128]. The implied terms as to correspondence with description or sample, fitness for purpose and satisfactory quality can only be excluded or restricted in so far as the term is reasonable[129]. This should therefore work in the customer's favour.

---

124 The Act does not apply to insurance contracts; the sale of land; contracts relating to companies; the sale of shares; and the carriage of goods by sea (Schedule 1); or to international supply contracts (s26).
125 S2(1) UCTA 1977 (UK).
126 S2(2) UCTA 1977 (UK).
127 S11(2) UCTA 1977 (UK).
128 S6(1) UCTA 1977 (UK).
129 S6(3) UCTA 1977 (UK).

9.5.3 The requirement of reasonableness

Under s11(1) of the UCTA 1977, the requirement of reasonableness is that *"the term shall have been a fair and reasonable one to be included having regard to the circumstances which were, or ought reasonably to have been, known to or in the contemplation of the parties when the contract was made."* Section 11(2) provides that, in determining whether the clause is a reasonable one, regard shall be had to the Guidelines set out in Schedule 2 of the Act[130]. Under s11(4) where the exclusion clause seeks to limit liability rather than exclude it completely, the court must have regard to two factors: the resources available to meet the liability, and the extent to which insurance cover was available to the party aiming to limit liability.

As has been stated earlier, it is quite common and reasonable for the customer to expect the service provider to have taken out insurance policies to cover direct losses, but these would be restricted to some ceiling for inconsequential losses. Under such circumstances it is feasible to assume that limitation clauses negotiated by the customer may be sustained by the courts – especially when contracting with larger, well resourced service providers.

The next chapter discusses the sensitive area of pricing within outsourcing contracts, and the need for flexibility.

[130] (1) The bargaining strengths of the parties relative to each other and the availability of alternative supplies, (2) Whether the customer received an inducement to agree to the term. (3) Whether the customer knew or ought reasonably to have known of the existence and extent of the term, (4) Where the term excludes or restricts any relevant liability if some condition is not complied with, whether it was reasonable at the time of the contract to expect that compliance with that condition would be practicable and (5) Whether the goods were manufactured, processed or adapted to the special order of the customer.

10. Pricing

This chapter discusses the types of pricing schemes that are prevalent in outsourcing deals, and how pricing clauses may need to be flexible in the context of unexpected changes to the environment or business models.

10.1 Types of pricing schema

Price is one of the major debating issues with offshore outsourcing. The rates[131] have a high degree of variability due to foreign exchange and labour market fluctuations. It is important to take advantage of cost reductions whilst also protecting against upward revision[132].

Traditionally, outsourcing contracts have relied upon strict price definitions, usually a simple "unit of service multiplied by price" model[133]. This model is disadvantageous as over time the interests of the two parties diverge, as the service provider consistently searches for methods to drive up the amount of service consumed by the customer, and the client increasingly searches for methods to reduce the units of service consumed and constantly shops around for a lower per unit rate service provider.

New pricing models are becoming based on a "gain sharing" principle, which attempts to ensure the interests of both parties are served in trying to improve performance. This may be through sharing of efficiency savings or credits for helping the service provider win new business.

---

[131] The pricing for services is usually defined in terms of rates per unit of usage.

[132] Crocker, K.J., S.E "Pretia Ex Machine? Prices & Process in Long Term Contracts", Journal of Law and Economics, Vol 34 (1991), 69-100.

[133] Either people employed (hours and days, categorised by skill level), or Resources em ployed (call centre workstations dedicated, machine cycles utilised, equipment hours expended and supplied consumed) or Events handled (customer calls taken / placed, units shipped, square feet cleaned, transactions processed etc).

10.1.1 Incentive pricing

There are numerous types of incentive pricing plans that are prevalent in outsourcing deals, these include:

- Incentive pricing based on milestones.
- Project specific gain share incentives e.g. a deal between the customer and service provider which requires each to invest a given percentage, with a sharing of savings between the parties in proportionate amounts equal to investment amounts.
- Shared pricing - in these deals, the service provider's remuneration is shared between a fixed price fee and an incentive fee. The incentive portion can be based on any number of metrics.
- Gainsharing - the provider receives a percentage of the improvement based on achieving or exceeding targets. There is no downside risk to the provider - the provider does not forfeit income for lower-than-expected improvements.
- Risk/reward - these incentive plans build on the gainsharing concept by adding the downside risk.

Increasingly, benchmarking is used to price services. This includes the provision to allow a third party to assess the pricing and performance of services provided under agreement relative to market figures. It also protects both parties if the industrial structure of the sector changes during contract term. It thus allows the sharing of cost savings.

Pricing incentives can be a simple tiered pricing where unit prices go down when volumes go up. This is the simplest form of providing motivation to both parties, and it is prevalent in most major outsourcing contracts. Gainsharing however is when both sides invest and then share any benefits that arise.

Customers need to accept that a service provider needs to make a "reasonable" profit (what is traditionally called its cost of capital). Customers should not try to decide whether a price is good for the service provider - each party should focus on what is acceptable to them.

Incentives only work with clearly defined service levels. Risk/reward arrangements are based on service level commitments. The process for defining incentives is relatively straightforward in theory - define the desired service level, then negotiate – however one must remember that the objective should be achieving the party's goal, not penalizing the service provider. In the process, it is also important to define clearly what is controllable by the service provider and thus the service level commitments are achievable in practice. Gainsharing should be reserved for deals with specific targets, so there are discernible links between cause and effect. Not all outsourcing deals should be gainsharing. Only when the conditions are favourable (incentives aligned and when both parties are willing to share risks) should gainsharing be given consideration.

10.1.2 Payments

Payment for services may be tied to formal acceptance criteria procedures set by the customer. This helps reassure the customer that it will receive services in a manner and time as required. In addition, payments may be tied to milestones with small percentage payments upon completion of each milestone.

Many outsourcing deals also have a provision for with-holding payments, pending a dispute or unsatisfactory performance by the service provider. Typically service providers require that customer places payments into an escrow account at the given date - this guards against temptations by the customer to with-hold payments for trivial issues or more cynically for its own cash flow management purposes.

10.1.3 Contracting for change

It is good practice (and in common with a partnership model) to ensure that non-material changes should not generate additional (or reduced) charges – this saves significant time and resources in not having to negotiate every change no matter how significant.

Any additional service provider charges should be determined on a net basis – i.e. net of any savings made or gains from economies of scale. This is the basis upon which a partnership model will survive – both parties must be seen to dealing with the other on a fair and equitable basis.

Adjustment to pricing should not be a one way process – if a change results in a reduction in the service provider's costs, a reduction in the charges may be appropriate.

In the case of significant non-recurring event, the parties should review and if appropriate adjust pricing. Following a significant non-recurring event, the pricing model reflected in the agreement may no longer serve to provide fair and equitable pricing – the contract should provide that if there is a significant non-recurring event, the parties will meet to review the provider's charges and to consider appropriate changes – the provision should also state that if the parties cannot reach agreement, then pricing will be equitably adjusted.

The next chapter discusses the area of transition of service provision from one service provider to another or repatriation of operations to the customer, when the contract expires or terminates.

11. Transition-in and change control

Good outsourcing contracts include specific commitments to support transition to another service provider, or repatriation of operations to the customer, when the contract expires or terminates. This chapter addresses what should be required at the outset of the relationship and how this should be managed.

11.1 Transition-in

An outsourcing deal requires the transfer of responsibility and possibly assets and employees from the customer to a service provider. In many cases the services that are outsourced are mission critical and small hiccups in service delivery can be disastrous, especially in the context of banks and other sectors transferring transaction processing functions to a service provider in India.

Unfortunately all too often, customers leave issues with respect to transition off the table and view these as "implementation issues" to be dealt with after contract signature.

In large scale outsourcing deals, where there is the transfer of staff, assets and possibly IP, the transition period can run into many months, requiring significant resources, time and effort from both parties – in some senses the transition period is actually a "test" period of the capability of the service provider – the final agreement on SLAs may not be practically possible before this "test" has been completed. It is therefore important to view the transition period, process and terms of reference for the transition, with equal if not more, importance than the longer term outsourcing contract.

Customers should insist on a preliminary transition plan before the contract is signed. Payments for transition-in related services should be contingent upon achievement of key milestones.

Good outsourcing contracts include specific commitments to support transition to another service provider, or repatriation of operations to the customer, when the contract expires or terminates. Required support often includes:

- Transfers of data, software and assets.
- Collaboration in the preparation and execution of transition plans.
- Familiarization of successor staff with operations and working documents.
- An opportunity for the customer (or a successor) to recruit dedicated or on-site staff.

11.2 Change control

Companies' business requirements are continually changing, as is the environment in which they operate. Given the length of time it can take to negotiate an outsourcing contract, the contract which is ultimately signed may not reflect all of the customer's original requirements. Within a short period of time after contract signature, it is likely that changes will be needed to reflect further differing requirements. Given this fact, outsourcing contracts need to contain a comprehensive mechanism by which the parties can agree the scope and charging impact of any particular change. The change control mechanism is likely to contain procedures for proposing and accepting changes, as well as an escalation process for resolving disputes over the scope and pricing of any change.

In the ordinary course, change control requires the agreement of both parties before a change will be effective. The procedure itself cannot usually force an agreement between the parties. In some limited circumstances, it may be appropriate for the parties to agree that the implementation of a change in scope will not be delayed by the inability of the parties to agree to the price associated with that change - For example, due to a significant stock market crash, a customer may suddenly require far lower volumes of service from its service provider.

In such circumstances, the contract might provide for the change to become effective immediately, with the pricing impact being negotiated after the event - E.g. a force majeure scenario, where regardless of the customer's disaster recovery provision, it will expect the supplier to move quickly and flexibly in responding to its needs.

11.3 Mergers

When a merger agreement is made, the typical reaction is for company "A" to force company "B" to get out of any existing deals and make them compatible with those of the acquirer. Under such circumstances, the functional relationship of company "B" are severely disrupted and often lost completely.

In order to avoid such a scenario, it is recommended that outsourcing parties incorporate appropriate provisions within the contract. These provisions should include mechanisms to deal with future mergers (including pricing for additional work), securing commitment from the outsourcing provider to use competitive pricing for the addition of merger volumes and anticipate and plan around problems related to the lack of information and lack of cooperation.

The next chapter discusses the issue of scope – frequently the area where most disputes arise.

12. Scope of services to be outsourced

Some consider scope as the single most important issue within an outsourcing contract. This chapter considers the factors which generally lead to disputes that arise in the context of scope creep and undisclosed assets. It also looks at the typical services that are outsourced and are therefore usually subject to the scope clauses.

12.1 Scope of the services contracted

Outsourcing agreements may have a number of services that form part of the contract. Where assets and employees are transferred, the range of services may be significant. However, there may be other services which are less obvious to definitively assert are part of the agreement. Where there is potential for disagreement, it is likely that some form of scope creep will be inevitable.

Sometimes it is the sheer complexity of services which leads to problems. Where large scale critical services are outsourced it may be implicitly assumed by the customer that low order, complementary services are also part of the agreement. The service provider on the other hand, may have only priced and contracted for the major critical services and the inclusion of these lesser services may make the contract unprofitable. It is therefore wise to ensure clearly the intentions of the customer in terms of services to be outsourced as part of the RFP process.

Scope which ultimately drives pricing may be the single most important issue. After signing the contract, scope is the most frequent issue of contention.

Well defined requirements, accurate cost data, full disclosure, and thorough investigation by the service provider, culminating in a precise well-drafted statement of work with clear limits, qualifications and exclusions will limit potential problems in the course of the contractual relationship.

12.1.1 General scope clauses[134]

General scope (or "sweep") clauses supplement detailed statements of work by obligating the service provider to perform:

- Lesser-included or inherent functions not specifically described but inherent in other functions described in general terms.
- Related functions formerly performed by displaced staff, or with assets.

Reasonable disclosure and investigation should give the service provider an opportunity to specify qualifications, limitations and exclusions. Thus, the actual scope for surprise should be reduced.

12.1.2 Undisclosed assets

Some scope issues concern assets, contracts or other resources omitted from contract documents and cost models, or overlooked by one or both sides.

Negotiated allocations of these risks vary, depending upon disclosures, leverage and other circumstances. One common resolution is an "unidentified resources" clause, sweeping into scope, matters that were disclosed, or should have been discovered, but obligating the customer to pay for additional resources, effort and services that were not disclosed, and could not have been anticipated.

12.1.3 Outsourced functions

Commercial companies as well as government agencies are increasingly considering outsourcing key functions. Although virtually any function can be outsourced, some have a better prospect than others. Figure 3 categories the types of services that are being outsourced dependent upon economies of skill and scope.

[134] Adapted from Allocating Risks in Outsourcing by George Kimball.

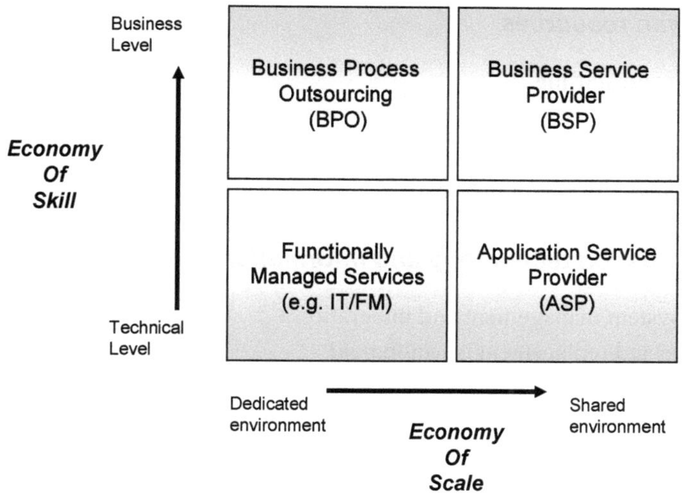

Fig.3. Types of outsourcing (Battenburg Model of outsourcing categories)

The major activities that are currently being outsourced include:

12.1.3.1 Administration

- Printing and reprographics
- Records management
- Administrative information systems
- Supply / inventory management

12.1.3.2 Customer service

- Telephone customer support
- Email customer support
- Customer service information systems

12.1.3.3 Finance

- Payroll processing
- Purchasing / invoicing
- General accounting

12.1.3.4 Human resources

- Recruitment and staffing
- Consulting
- Training
- Human resource information systems

12.1.3.5 Information technology and information systems

- Legacy IT system management and integration
- Maintenance and replacement of equipment
- IT systems upgrade
- IT systems management
- E-commerce
- Project management

12.1.3.6 Real estate

- Security management
- Facilities management and maintenance
- Facilities information systems

12.1.3.7 Logistics

- Warehousing and freight audit
- Distribution and logistics
- Fleet management, operations and maintenance

The next chapter examines the necessity for Service Level Agreements (SLAs), and provides guidance on choosing appropriate metrics and how these should be measured and incorporated into a contract.

13. Service Level Agreements

A Service Level Agreement (SLA) is an essential part of any outsourcing project. It defines the boundaries of the project in terms of the functions and services that the service provider will give to its client, the volume of work that will be accepted and delivered and the quality of deliverables. This chapter discusses SLAs in detail, providing guidance on choosing appropriate metrics and how these should be measured and incorporated into a contract.

13.1 Type of Service Level Agreements

The typical outsourcing engagement will last for a number of years and be governed by a contract setting the terms and conditions between the client and outsourcer for the duration of their relationship. To measure whether that relationship is working, and how well, SLAs are established.

A service level agreement describes the performance levels required of the service provider of each service or product provided by the service provider. Performance standards can be extensive if a customer wants to manage processes, or they can be limited to a few key standards if the relationship is purely results based. SLAs are usually incorporated as a schedule to the contract.

An SLA is an essential part of any outsourcing project. It defines the boundaries of the project in terms of the functions and services that the service provider will give to its client, the volume of work that will be accepted and delivered, the acceptance of criteria that will be used and a level of quality for deliverables. Well defined SLAs correctly set expectations for both sides of the relationship and provides targets for accurately measuring performance to those objectives.

They act not only as metrics of performance by which to measure the service provider's performance but also as a means of providing both parties with meaningful information on which to base fees, costs, remedies, and performance incentives and disincentives.

It is a general expectation, encouraged by the industry and the trade bodies that have formed around the issue of service levels that the Service Level Agreement (SLA) represents the service level that will be delivered. This, unfortunately, is a myth. If an SLA sets a threshold at the same level as the average performance of a service then the supplier will, by definition, fail to meet it half of the time.

There are few service providers who would consciously enter into a contract that caused them to fail at this rate. In practice, the SLA, when entered into by entities who understand the process, defines a level of performance at which the service provider will accept the risk of failure. This means that the actual delivered performance should be better than the SLA threshold by an amount that defines the risk. The gap between the two is a statistical value that depends on the population of services, the measurement time and the rate at which failures occur. There is no single relationship between these parameters and that is where the value of a dynamic risk assessment model enters into the business equation.

The recent history of SLAs is unfortunately littered with examples that did not lead to the expected outcome for either party. Common mistakes include:

- Setting the target thresholds to the average of a series of actual measures.
- Setting such complex SLAs that custom billing systems are needed to operate them.
- Setting unnecessary targets that affect the design out of proportion to the performance requirement.
- Including measures that have never been used before and which have little, if any, impact on the service delivered to the end users of the services.
- Specifying measures in such fine detail, or over such a short period, that it is impossible to achieve statistical significance in the measures (this makes the risk almost unquantifiable).

13.2 Performance standards

The performance standards and service levels specified depend upon the type of service being measured and the relevant phase of the agreement (e.g., during the initial transition period service levels may be lower than during steady state).

The performance can be measured either on a subjective basis or on more objective basis. It is no surprise that lawyers for the service provider would prefer more subjective standards, where there is more wriggle room.

Subjective performance standards may include (but are not limited to):

- Use of reasonable efforts in providing the services.
- Use of best efforts in providing the services.
- Performance of the services in a professional and workmanlike manner or in accordance with industry standards. Clearly the difficulty arises in defining

"industry standard". This would most probably entail some form of benchmarking or assessment of some quality standard. However, a quality standard such as the ISO 9001 standard merely provides reassurance that the service provider has documented various processes – it is not a guarantee of the quality of its output.

Objective standards may include (but are not limited to):

- Conformance to specifications.
- Conformance to baseline operational performance metrics.
- Conformance to service levels previously attained by the customer or a third party provider for the same services.
- Conformance to benchmarked operational standards and service levels.

13.3 Process and Quality standards

Quality is a major concern with offshore outsourcing. Defects are more costly to fix than requirement problems. A strict quality assurance and control program forms an integral part of every offshore delivery model. Offshore projects and delivery centres are assessed using different methodologies:

- A CMM (Capability Maturity Model) assessment that measures the quality of an organization's management and software engineering practices. CMM defines a number of levels of process maturity (from Level 1 - initial, through Level 2 - repeatable, up to Level 4 - managed and Level 5 - optimised). Assessment is derived from a series of questions (over 120 of them) set in terms of project activities that should be carried out, standards that should be in place and abilities that should be evident.
- ISO 9001 - 2000 certification - a basic framework for process control. Based on the maxim "Say what you do, do what you say" - an international standard for quality management systems maintained by the International Organization of Standardization.
- ISO 15504 - a complement to ISO 9001 that identifies key process areas and assesses their effectiveness. Once known as SPICE, ISO 15504 is used to improve processes, especially those between separate business units.
- Six Sigma process improvement methodologies - Performance management involves, among other things, a review and continuous improvement of software development and business processes. Six Sigma focuses on business process improvement. It is a quality measurement and improvement program that focuses on the control of a process six sigma (standard deviations) from the mean.

13.4 Rules for effective SLAs

Ensuring that the customer has defined an effective SLA is crucial to the performance of the relationship over the many years the agreement will run for. Unfortunately SLAs tend to be defined and incorporated into the agreement by lawyers. For all the benefits that lawyers bring to the table, defining effective SLAs is not usually one of them. SLAs should be designed by the people who run the business at the operational level - after all, most of the outsourced services are at the operational level, not at the executive level. It is also important to understand how a particular parameter is to be measured and whether measurements can have some statistical significance attached to them – otherwise the management of the SLA is likely to get complex and difficult.

Having ruled out lawyers as experts in the design and definition of SLAs, it is also worth noting that engineers solely responsible is also likely to cause some difficulty down path. Although probably stereotypical, engineers tend to overcomplicate the process, introducing too many measures - sometimes the 80/20 rule is important in designing effective SLAs. Only those parts of the process which can be controlled directly should form part of the SLA – including service levels which are too disaggregated, or cannot be controlled or which are a derivative of another process cannot be considered as effective SLAs.

The six rules of an effective SLA:

1. Is it simple?
2. Is the measure the whole parameter you need?
3. Can the measured parameter be controlled?
4. Is the measured parameter a primary measure or a derivative?
5. Is the measurement of the parameter a part of a control loop?
6. Does the measurement period provide statistical significance?

If the answer is always yes then you probably have a good parameter to measure.

In addition, for SLAs to be effective, it is a fundamental requirement for there to be a full, clear, complete and documented service specification. This is usually not an issue with most outsourcing agreements, but what is usually not defined is a full, clear, complete and documented process specification.

Ideally, there should be a clear statement of key targets, supported by sound product documentation.

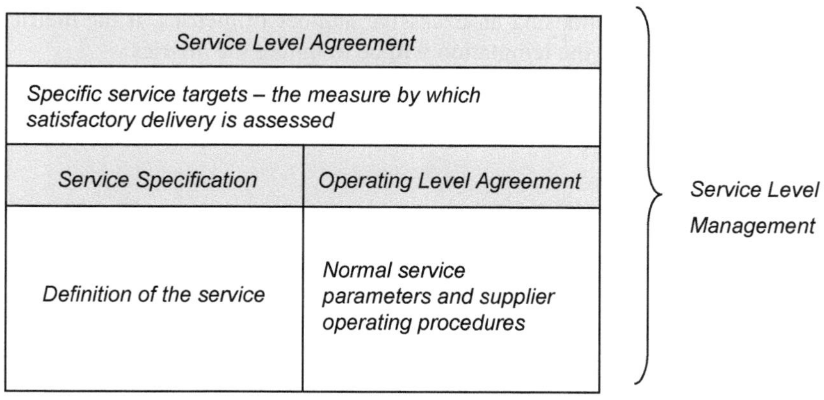

Fig.4. Contents of a service level agreement

In practice, it is often the case that everything is bundled into the SLA, resulting in a large and complex document where the underlying documentation is absent, resulting in an SLA that is open to broad interpretation.

13.5 Selecting appropriate metrics

Selecting the appropriate metrics to gauge project performance is a critical step for any outsourcing engagement. The selection process is complicated by the large number of potential metrics and must be tempered by considerations such as organisational experience, the type of behaviours to be motivated and cost and effort of collection.

Key principles to bear in mind include[135]:

- Choose measurements that motivate the right behaviour – each side must understand the other side, its expectations and its goals, and the factors that are within their respective control.
- Ensure metrics reflect factors within the service provider's control – the metric should be two sided. If the service provider's ability to meet objectives is dependent on an action from the customer, the customer performance must also be measured.
- Choose measurements that are easily collected – If the metrics in the SLA cannot be easily collected, then they will eventually be ignored.

[135] Metrics for IT Outsourcing Service Level Agreements, Clarity Consulting Inc 2004, by Ian. S. Hayes.

- Less is more – Avoid choosing an excessive number of metrics, if the metrics generate too much data, the temptation will be to ignore the metrics.
- Set a proper baseline – To be useful, metrics must be set to reasonable, attainable performance levels. This is where benchmarking may be a useful tool (discussed later).

Typical major categories of SLAs include:

- Volume of work – typically the key sizing determinant of an outsourcing project.
- Quality of work – tend to be the most diverse of all SLA metrics – it may be appropriate that each major deliverable contained in a SLA has a corresponding acceptance criteria to judge the quality of the deliverable[136].
- Responsiveness – these metrics measure the amount of time that it takes for an outsourcer to handle a client request[137].
- Efficiency – measures the engagement's effectiveness at providing services at a reasonable cost[138].

13.6 Measurement and management

Having established appropriate metrics, which are controllable, manageable and motivate the right behaviour, it is important to examine and document a "metric measurement and management" process as part of the outsourcing agreement. As the name implies, what is needed is a "process" as opposed to some add-on or bolt-on procedure for metric measurement. The process must be designed so it is fit for purpose. Fig 5 below illustrates the design flow that the outsourcing service provider and customer must jointly design and agree.

---

136 I.e. defect rates, standards compliance, technical quality, service availability, service satisfaction.

137 I.e. time to market or time to implement, time to acknowledgement or backlog size.

138 I.e. cost / effort efficiency, team utilisation, rework levels.

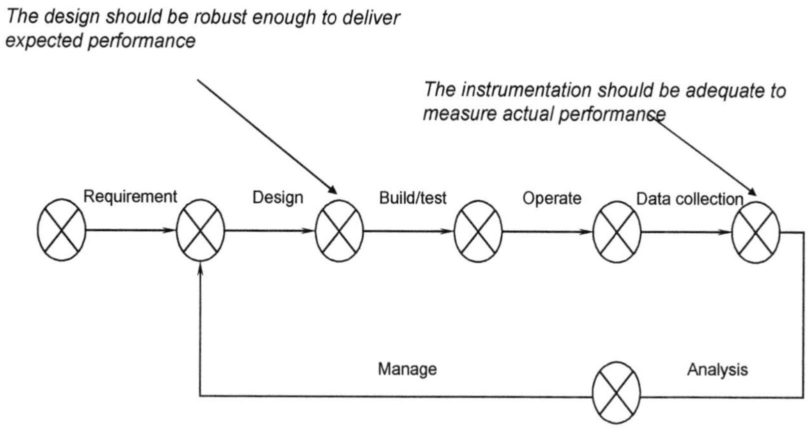

Fig. 5. Design flow for a measurement system

13.6.1 Collecting process information

A key part of measurement and management is the collection of process information. The delivery of a particular service involves a process, where at each step, certain data / information will be presented, before the next step in the process can start or continue. It is important to identify which data / information at each step in the process is required to be collected and reported as part of the SLA. Fig 6 illustrates the typical process and data collection points for an "order fulfilment process".

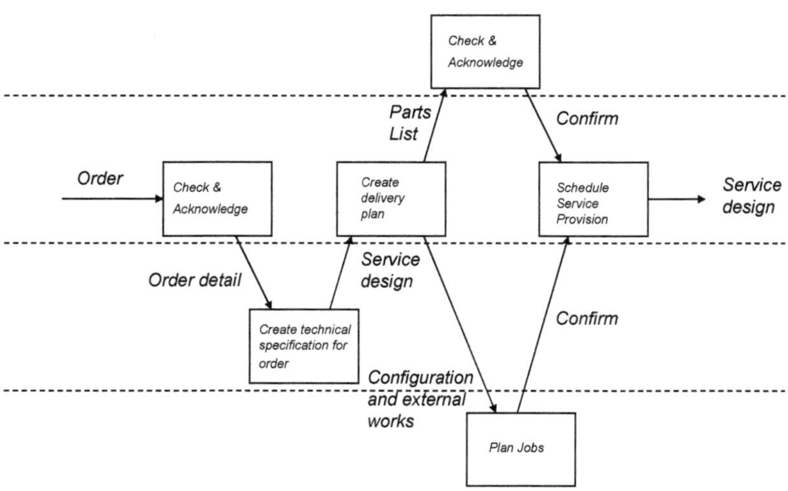

Fig. 6. Example of a data fulfilment information collection process

13.6.2 Reporting

The final routine function as part of the measurement and management process is the format and frequency of the reporting obligations. Parties should be clear about which metrics should be reported as part of the SLA and which should be reported separately, if needed, for operational reasons. Those that are reported as part of the SLA management system should be simple and concise, whilst operational reporting may be more extensive and shared at the operational level between the parties as a mechanism to improve the process or systems over time.

In many senses what is useful for management purposes is a "dashboard" of key metrics which combine pure SLA metrics and some operational metrics which could explain the reasons for the divergence of service delivery targets and therefore aid in understanding what changes should be implemented by the service provider – sharing this information with the customer will reassure them that indeed both parties are working under a partnership model and the service provider is doing what is can to improve performance. Fig 7 illustrates a typical format for reporting obligations:

Monthly review	*SLA review*	*Trends*
- summary of performance against SLA targets over the current period	*- are the targets still in line with customer need and supplier capability*	*- alarm bells and immediate restorative action planning*
- facts behind the figures *- agreement of credits (if any) and actions required.*	*- if there is a need or desire to change, what steps have to be taken to make it happen*	*- input to long term planning (e.g. ordering of more network capacity, increase in support staff)*

Fig. 7. Typical reporting obligations

13.7 Benchmarking

Historically one mechanism used to ensure meaningful cost savings for the customer has been the insertion of a "most favoured customer" pricing clauses – however these are difficult to apply and do not necessarily bring about the best price for the customer, and thus there has been a movement towards benchmarking.

Benchmarking is a process whereby a metric set for services performed to particular service levels, is compared to a sample of metrics by other organisations for similar services. Particularly for larger contracts, this process is normally carried out by an independent, third party benchmarking organisation.

The general purpose of such a provision is to permit a party to the contract to initiate a process by which the parties' contractual pricing for services or service level agreements are benchmarked against comparable situations. The contractual provision will normally require adjustments in the contract pricing or service levels to the benchmarked level. At the contract stage, much of the negotiation of benchmarking involves agreement to a structure for the procedure and the type of information that will be used in the analysis.

The contract will need to state which party may initiate a benchmarking exercise, when it may be initiated and who the bench marker will be. The parties usually agree "substantial change" provision that addresses the parties' respective rights in cases where there are substantial increases or decreases in the outsourced services. The parties should also decide when the benchmark will be triggered – usually the parties will limit the frequency of a benchmarking to once per annum.

The provisions for selecting the bench marker may be structured several ways:

- Specify one or more bench markers by name and allow the customer to select from the list.
- Require that they both mutually agree on the bench marker – the provision may include examples of the type of bench marker they would choose.

The scope of the benchmark will often require a great deal of negotiation by the parties, to enable a like for like comparison (factors included in the benchmarking procedure to ensure normalization of the results to the particular situation being studied).

Having undertaken a benchmarking study, the parties will need to decide how the results are to be handled. These will typically lead to some form of dispute. Normally the preferred method is to include a contract provision for an internal dispute resolution procedure involving one or more joint operating and executive committees. In the case of benchmarking, the disputes are typically the failure of the parties to reach agreement based on a range of possible choices – the dispute is not a legal dispute.

13.8 Remedies as part of the SLA

The agreement should specify what remedies will be available to the customer in the event the service provider fails to meet a service level. The agreement should also specify whether one or more of the remedies is exclusive (i.e., to the exclusion of other remedies).

In an ideal world the assumptions / penalty consequences process would take place before the system is designed so that the results could be included in the design. In many cases this does not happen and the SLAs are set in the contract such that the system has to be designed to meet them at an acceptable risk level without any opportunity for trade-offs.

Unexcused failures to meet critical service levels may obligate the service provider to pay liquidated damages (credits, or penalties). Their purpose is deterrent, rather than compensatory, since the amounts are rarely sufficient to compensate for serious disruptions in service.

Service providers generally impose a ceiling upon credit payments roughly corresponding to their anticipated margin.

Repeated failures may be classified as "unacceptable service" that constitutes "material breach" and justifies default termination.

In practice, service levels leave most of the risk with the customer. Even substantial credits rarely provide full compensation for serious disruptions. The actual importance of service levels may be less than commonly supposed. Service providers never commit to meet service levels that they cannot consistently achieve. However, service levels reassure customers that service commitments have "teeth". They focus the service provider's attention on key systems and services, so that commitments are met.

Service providers fear abuse of SLAs, and the possibility that they may not be paid, even when obliged to perform. These differences are commonly reconciled through:

- Commitments to continue both payment and performance while disputes are pending.
- Limitations upon the amount that can be withheld from any single invoice (commonly expressed as a percentage of base charges).
- Obligations to place larger disputed amounts in escrow[139], pending resolution of the dispute.

Many customers are increasingly looking at new models for implementing SLAs. In the performance decrement model for instance, the emphasis is on making sure the service provider corrects problems in a timely manner rather than generating credits that are inconsequential to both the service provider and customer.

---

[139] a trust account held in the borrower's name to pay obligations.

In the performance decrement model, the service provider does not use the customer's existing in-house service level performance to arrive at the service provider's required performance. Traditional SLAs typically allow the service provider to merely meet the customer's performance levels, because there is no other data to rely upon. In the performance decrement model, the customer requires the service provider to propose performance standards that are consistent with industry best practices.

If the total amount of performance decrement points assessed in a given cumulative period exceeds a certain threshold, then a mandatory meeting is convened of the parties' executive committee. The service provider is required to propose a solution to the failures.

If the total amount of performance decrements assessed in a given cumulative period exceeds the second threshold, the customer has a contractual right to require that the service provider pay for a customer selected outsourcing "consultancy" to perform an analysis and determine the reasonable fees for the service provider's relative performance standards.

If the total amount of performance decrement assessed in a given cumulative period exceeds the third threshold, the customer has at its sole discretion to either modify or terminate one or more of the services or modify or terminate the entire agreement for cause. Clearly the number and level of thresholds is a debating matter.

The next chapter delves into the heart of most outsourcing agreements - certainly from the customer perspective – the proper allocation of responsibilities and obligations to meet stated performance standards during the term of the outsourcing agreement and the remedies for non-performance.

14. Contract enforcement

The fundamental principle for an outsourcing agreement is proper allocation of responsibilities and obligations to meet stated performance standards during the term of the outsourcing agreement. However, it is likely that the service provider may not meet all its obligations. The chapter discusses the various remedies that can be included in the contract, such as liquidated damages and credits to motivate and compensate for non performance.

14.1 Typical remedies for failures to perform obligations

It is foreseeable that a service provider will not perform all its obligations or meet all performance standards during the term of the outsourcing agreement. Imposing damages is a common remedy, but measuring damages for failures to perform obligations and meet performance standards can be difficult.

There are various methods by which remedies can be imposed:

- Credits - credits awarded for each failure of the service provider to meet each performance measurement.
- Additional equipment and software at no cost or at wholesale cost.
- Liquidated damages – although disliked by service providers, liquidated damages are possible to obtain in outsourcing agreements. They need to be carefully and narrowly crafted and be very specific to have the likelihood of being included and enforced as part of the agreement.

Key ways to limit liability - specifically used by service providers (except liability for death and personal injury which cannot be excluded or limited[140]) include (but not limited to):

- Exclusion of implied terms.
- Exclusion of consequential / indirect loss.

---

[140] E.g. UCTA 1977 (UK) and the EU Unfair Contract Terms Directive (93/13/EEC) - Member States must make sure that effective means exist under national law to enforce these rights and that such terms are no longer used by businesses. All Member States were required to implement the Directive into their national law by 31 December 1994.

- Use of liquidated ascertained damages / limit on each and aggregate financial liability.
- Exclusion of loss contributed by other party / third party.
- Creation of compensation options such as right to replace a service.

Contract law generally entitles one party to terminate a contract if the other party "materially breaches" the contract. A breach that isn't "material" may entitle one party to claim damages, but will not entitle that party to terminate the contract. Identifying the "critical" factors which constitute material breach is essential.

Terms may create strict liabilities, or merely liability for negligence. Strict liability can arise even if there is no "fault" - it makes no difference that you tried your best.

In liability for negligence, there is a duty to perform certain contract obligations with reasonable care and skill - duties to take reasonable care can also be imposed in tort.

Generally, the remedy for a breach of contract is an award of damages. In some exceptional cases, it may be possible to specifically enforce the contract, or to seek an injunction to prevent some breach of it occurring. Where a court grants specific performance or an injunction, these are both discretionary forms of relief, based on equitable jurisdiction. In many cases, damages are intended to be compensatory in nature, and the basis of assessment is loss to the claimant, rather than gain to the defendant.

Damages are a common law remedy and are available as a right if a breach of contract has been proved. Where no loss results from the breach to the claimant, an award of nominal damages may be made. If loss has resulted, the court must then determine the basis of calculation of the award. It may take account of a number of different types of harm.

Broadly, the court is aiming to put the claimant into the position he would have been in if the contract had been properly performed. To achieve this, the court must:

- Identify the harm flowing from the breach which is not too remote.
- Then establish the quantum or measure of damages appropriate to that harm .

14.1.1 Basis for assessment of damages

- Claiming for reliance loss - the cost to the claimant of relying on the contract.
- Claiming for restitution loss - the value of the benefit conferred on the defendant by the claimant.

- Claiming for expectation loss - putting the claimant into the position he would have been in if the contract had been properly performed.

It is possible to claim under more than one of these heads provided that there is no double compensation as a result.

14.1.2 Duty to mitigate

The party injured by a breach of contract is under a duty to take reasonable steps to mitigate his losses. He cannot be compensated if, in mitigating his loss, he manages to make a better deal[141].

14.1.3 Liquidated damages and penalty clauses

Damages assessed by the court are called unliquidated damages. If the parties choose to put a term in their contract, fixing for certain sums to be paid in the event of specified breaches of contract, these are liquidated damages. If the sums fixed are not found to be a genuine pre-estimate of likely loss, the clause in question may be found to be a penalty clause. Tests to assist in distinguishing liquidated damages clauses from penalty clauses were developed by the House of Lords in Dunlop Pneumatic Tyre Co v New Garage & Motor Co [1915] AC 79. A penalty clause will only be enforced by the court to the extent commensurate with the loss sustained[142].

14.2 Damages available in India

Damages are pecuniary compensation recoverable in law, by a person who has sustained some damages by the act or fault of another, whether such an act or fault is a breach of contract or a tort.

The term 'damages' in its legal sense, means the compensation which the law will award for an injury done[143]. It is a comprehensive term, including compensation for the default of the party charged therewith, and all the factors going to make up the total amount which the plaintiff may recover under correct principles of law. But in its ordinary acceptation, Indian courts are opposed to awards of previously fixed compensation[144].

---

141 Banco de Portugal v Waterlow [1932] AC 452 and British Westinghouse v Underground Electric Railways [1912] AC 673.

142 Jobson v Johnson [1989] 1 All ER 621.

143 It could include recompense or satisfaction in money for a loss or injury sustained.

144 Conversation with Sajai Advocates, Bangalore, India.

14.2.1 General damages

Damages to person or to property are either general or special. In cases of breach of contract, general damages are such damages as the law implies or presumes from the breach complained of. Such damages, as arise naturally in the usual course of things from such breach, and which may reasonably be supposed to have been in the contemplation of the parties.

14.2.2 Special damages

Special damages are those which are the natural, but not the necessary consequences of the wrong.

They may be the actual result in a particular circumstance of a case from the wrong, but are not a necessary consequence that will be implied by the law or will be deemed to have been within the contemplation of the parties. They arise out of an unusual or peculiar state of facts, which may be known to one of the parties but not to the other. The damages follow the wrong, as natural and proximate consequences in the particular case, by reason of special circumstances or conditions.

14.2.3 Distinction between general and special damages in contract

The distinction between 'General' and 'Special' damages is that the former are such damages as the law implies, or presumes from the breach, while the latter are such as have proximately resulted, but do not always immediately result from the breach and are not therefore implied by law.

14.2.4 Exemplary damages

In general, actual damages must be shown to recover exemplary damages, but exemplary damages cannot be awarded in an action for breach of contract, since the existence of misconduct cannot alter the rule, by which the damages for breach of contract are assessed. Section 73 of the Contract Act 1872 does not warrant such an award. It provides that: "When a contract has been broken, the party who suffers by such breach is entitled to receive, from the party who has broken the contract, compensation for any loss or damage caused to him thereby, which naturally arose in the usual course of things from such breach, or which the parties knew, when they made the contract, to be likely to result from the breach of it". Such compensation is however not given for any remote and indirect loss or damage sustained by reason of the breach.

Thus, exemplary damages are awarded in tort but not in contract[145]; because the defendant's motives and conduct are not to be taken into account in assessing damages[146] and damages are not to be awarded in respect of disappointment or wounded feelings.

The next chapter discusses in detail relevant provisions that must be thought through and incorporated within the contract for contract termination, including the various triggers that are commonly used for contract termination proceedings.

145 Rookes v. Barnard [1964] AC 1129 as per Lord Devlin at page 407.; Cassell & Co. Ltd v. Broome [1972] AC 1027.

146 Y.China Rattayya v. Donepudi Venkataramayya, AIR 1959 AP 551.

15. Contract termination procedures

Many companies suffer because they do not plan for what happens when the end date of the contract approaches. Companies usually omit to include a definition of procedures to be followed and assets allocated when the contract terminates. This chapter discusses what provisions should be included for contract termination, what the triggers for termination should be, and the transition of services from the terminated service provider back-into the company or another service provider.

15.1 The outsourcing lifecycle

Outsourcing needs to be treated like a project; it has a start, life and an end. Many customers suffer because they do not plan for what happens when the end date of the contract approaches[147]. Companies usually omit to include a definition of procedures to be followed and assets allocation when the contract terminates.

The outsourcing contract must define clearly what happens at the point of termination. The effects of termination often depend on the cause of termination (e.g., if one of the parties is in breach of the agreement). The agreement should give the parties a chance to decide how to wind down the relationship at a time when they are not involved in a dispute and are probably more inclined to be reasonable.

15.2 Triggers for termination

Whilst no one wants to consider the possibility of failure at the start of the relationship, it's crucial for both parties to a contract to have an effective exit strategy to avoid the possibility of being tied into an unfavourable deal. There are several reasons why a party might want to terminate an outsourcing contract early. Common triggers for contract termination include:

---

147 Sears, Roebuck & Co. ("Sears") exited its 10-year $1.6 billion IT outsourcing agreement with Computer Science Corp. ("CSC") after 11 months. Now the companies are disputing the grounds of the cancellation and whether Sears has to pay termination fees to CSC. In its motions filed with the US Court of Appeals in Chicago, CSC argued that Sears terminated the agreement "for convenience due to change in control" as a result of its merger with Kmart Holding Corp.

1. Failure to achieve objectives - where the customer chooses to terminate the contract because expected obligations have not been met by the service provider.
2. Expiration of term of contract.
3. Adverse action by government entities - where the outsourcing deal depends on a favourable government environment, such as licenses and approvals, tax incentives etc – especially relevant in the case of India.
4. Material default by either party.
5. Disputes - even after proceeding along a defined dispute resolution process it may be a valid action to exit the agreement.
6. Change in control - a change in control of the service provider or its parent company.
7. Change in company strategy, e.g. to bring the service back in-house - in these circumstances it is usually appropriate to arrange adequate financial compensation to cover the costs of the affected service provider.
8. Either party going out of business.
9. Failing to meet financial covenants.
10. Bankruptcy.
11. Incapacitated by Force Majeure events.

Transitioning away from a service provider involves considerable cost, risk and disruption. For this reason smart customers sharply restrict the service provider's right to terminate, usually only upon sustained failure to pay undisputed amounts.

15.3 Effects of termination or expiration / reversion clauses

As with many aspects of an outsourcing contract, it is difficult to predict with certainty what the environment on the ground will look like at some indeterminate point in the future. No matter how much detail is put in the contract about what is to happen to people or assets on termination, it's important to recognise this fact. The contract should contain a mechanism for developing and agreeing an exit plan covering these issues, and this will need to be updated on a regular basis.

The rights and duties of each of the parties upon termination or expiration of the agreement should depend upon the circumstances of the termination.

The agreement should set out the processes the parties will follow upon termination so that the transition is orderly. Some issues to consider include:

1. Whether the parties will need to return materials to the other party.
2. Whether there will be any ongoing license fees or other payment obligations.
3. Whether the customer will have the right to purchase equipment or other assets or to be assigned any equipment leases.

4. Whether the service provider or the customer will be responsible for effecting the transition of the transferred employees to the customer or a third party.

The parties should include a matrix in the agreement that shows what terms will apply for each type of termination, and include the following at the very least:

1. Ownership of any proprietary information, technology or other intellectual property created under the agreement.
2. Application of a termination fee, if appropriate.
3. Responsibility for demobilisation and remobilisation costs.
4. Obligations under non-solicitation, non-poaching and non-competition covenants in the agreement, if actually enforceable in India.
5. Ownership in any assets used, transferred or acquired during the term of the agreement.
6. Transition of any seconded or other employees back to the customer.

It is not unusual for a termination for convenience provision to include restrictions designed to inhibit exercise of the right, e.g. unenforcement of the customer's right to exercise the convenience termination in the first two or three years of the outsourcing contract term and in cases of M&A, a requirement for adequate notice to be given within a short period following acquisition event. Customers are not the only ones that can be acquired. Customers often negotiate certain rights and restrictions to address an acquisition of the outsourcer. Typical provisions will either require customer's consent to the outsourcer's assignment of the contract to the acquirer or will grant a favourable termination right to the customer if the sale occurs without the customer's consent through a merger or sale of stock of the outsourcer.

15.3.1 Transition-out services

Termination transition-out services are those additional services the service provider may undertake to provide upon expiration or termination of the outsourcing agreement. Some issues to consider include:

1. The amount, duration and type of termination transition-out services that may be provided may vary depending upon the reason for termination (e.g., termination services provided upon termination for the customer's convenience should differ from those provided upon termination due to the customer's breach).
2. The duration that the service provider will provide termination transition services to the customer.
3. The need for confidentiality agreements should the customer want to effect a transition from the services to a third party service provider (including an agreement that the third party's outsourcing division will not communicate the

service provider's confidential information or proprietary methodology to personnel in other divisions of the third party).

4. Payment.
5. Relief, if any, from service level and other performance obligations.

From a risk management perspective, the consequences of termination are as important as the triggers for termination. A customer wants the ability to take back its operations in-house, or transfer them to an alternative service provider, with the minimum of hassle and with adequate support from the outgoing service provider. This may involve the transfer of assets, third party contracts, licences and people. The customer needs the contract to set out the principles associated with such exit assistance and also an obligation on the outgoing service provider to co-operate.

In some cases, the service provider may not be in a position to provide quality transition service, and the customer may be able to reduce risk by structuring the deal to allow an easy exit without termination assistance. A contract that is "built for exit" might require the service provider to:

- Continue to use facilities, software, equipment and subcontractors that the customer owns or have a right to use.
- Provide the customer with traditionally internal information, such as the home phone numbers of any key personnel.
- Implement a mirrored disaster recovery site for the customer's work specifically and a disaster recovery plan that the customer can implement if the service provider's facility were to be destroyed.
- Cooperative with the customer in building internal capability or outside relationships to provide the same services that the outsourcer provides.

15.4 Dispute resolution mechanisms

The agreement needs a dispute resolution process. Quickly escalating disputes up the chain of management often resolves problems prior to litigation. Pending resolution of the dispute, however, the service provider should continue performing its services. If the parties cannot resolve the dispute within a pre-defined time period, either one should be entitled to pursue its other available remedies.

15.5 Escalation procedures

Escalation procedures are processes set up to define the steps taken when service levels do not meet service standards. This may involve determining fault for missed measures, reporting, problem resolution within a specified time and when the problem still isn't resolved, intervention on both the customer and service provider side.

The agreement should always strive to make decisions and address issues at the lowest possible level, however, when a resolution cannot be made, the item should be escalated to ensure a decision is made before it can impact upon the outsourcing agreement.

The following information should to be included as part of an escalation process:

- Items subject to the escalation process, including examples.
- The level of escalation and the number of participants in each level e.g. level 1: project manager / contract manager, level 2: departmental directors / legal, level 3: Senior executive / legal (more than three levels is usually discouraged).
- Who has the final decision on the dispute?
- Required time frames between escalation levels. These must be commensurate with the item being escalated and impact to the agreement if the item is not resolved.

The next chapter examines the relatively complex area of dual legal authorities and necessity to ensure that the contract and indeed the deal is structured with full appreciation of the fact that some aspects of the deal may be governed by Indian Laws.

16. Unenforceable contract terms under Indian legal system

It is important that companies understand that clauses addressing certain issues cannot be governed by any other selected law other than Indian Law. This chapter discusses some of the more important terms which can only be governed by Indian Law.

16.1 Sovereignty

Most countries preserve their sovereign rights under International law. Although the contract may state the governing law for the contract, and most countries accept International / Foreign Judgments as India does, there will be certain national legal procedures and laws which the sovereign country will not allow to be governed by any other national law.

It is therefore important that companies contemplating outsourcing to India understand that clauses addressing certain issues cannot be governed by any other selected law[148].

What are provided herein are only limited examples of the specific legal issue that companies should consider. It is strongly recommended that companies seek independent legal counsel from reputable Indian Law firms before proceeding with the outsourcing deal.

16.2 Indian statutes cannot be overwritten by any other law

Clauses addressing certain issues cannot be governed by any other selected Law, and have to be governed by Indian Law. These include issues relating to IP transfer, registration and protection, real estate, labour law and bankruptcy. All of the above identified areas have statutes governing them in India. Therefore the parties cannot by contract exclude the applicability of the statutes. For example, if a UK

---

148 i.e. they have to be governed by Indian Law.

Company sets up a captive delivery centre in India, which handles its software maintenance services. The UK Company will be governed by Indian laws in so far as the captive centre is concerned. While staffing the centre, again Indian laws will be applicable.

The same is the case in an outsourcing contract where a UK customer outsources work to an Indian service provider. Though the contract may be governed by UK law, for all functions carried out in India and all property based in India, Indian laws will be applicable. For example the staff of the Indian service provider will be governed by Indian Labour Laws. The contract cannot say that employees of the Indian service provider will not be allowed holidays which are statutory holidays. It should be noted that India has fairly stringent Labour Laws. The Industrial Disputes Act[149] lays down various rules and regulations regulating the conditions of employment of a certain category of workmen. The Act however does not apply to employees engaged in managerial or administrative work or employed in a supervisory capacity and drawing wages exceeding a stipulated amount.

In the same manner, Indian Law provides that for copyright to vest with the author it is sufficient if the work is original and is fixed on any medium (such as paper, floppy etc)[150]. The contract cannot say that copyright will vest with the UK Company upon creation by the employee. The copyright will vest with the employee who is the author unless it is assigned to the UK Company upon creation. Therefore the UK Company has to make sure that the Indian employee assigns the copyright to it in order to get all the IPR in the work.

As has been demonstrated, Indian Laws in all the above situations cannot be excluded by contract between the parties and the customer must be careful in drafting the contract, even where the governing law for the contract may be stipulated to be a European law. It is also because of these specific issues and in some situations knowledge of appropriate case law within India which may enable creative drafting of contract terms to the benefit of the customer, that the services of both an Indian and Domestic law firm is sought.

16.3 Non-predation clauses

Typically because of the risk that the service provider may become tomorrow's competitor, customers consider a set of non-predation clauses designed to protect from such competition from the service provider. Such provisions may include a non-solicitation covenant relating to the customer's current, recent and prospective customers. Protective covenants may also be appropriate to cover the ownership of IP developed in connection with the outsourcing contract, assuring at least the

149 Industrial Dispute Act, 1947 (India).

150 The Copyright Act, 1957 (India).

continued ability of the customer to make use of such innovation – if not securing outright ownership of them. However agreements in restraint of trade are deemed void in India. Every agreement by which anyone is restrained from exercising a lawful profession, trade or business of any kind, is to that extent void. The exception appears to be only an agreement not to carry on business of which goodwill is sold[151].

The next chapter discusses what has become an increasingly sensitive issue within the outsourcing industry, that of data protection and privacy. With a discussion on the relevant laws in this area and the measures that can be applied to ensure compliance.

151 Section 27, Indian Contract Act, 1872.

17. The EU Data Protection Directive 97/66/EC and related issues

Companies need to ensure that adequate data protection measures are applied and that the company is compliant with relevant Data protection Laws. This chapter discusses the relevant laws in this area and what measures can be applied to ensure compliance.

17.1 The requirement for data protection

Outsourcing agreements often involve the processing of large volumes of personal information about a company's customers or employees. In many cases, this information includes sensitive information, such as financial data, medical data, payroll and benefits information, social security numbers and purchasing histories. It is therefore very important to note that in many cases there is a legal obligation for the customer to protect such data.

17.2 Non disclosure agreements / confidentiality

Each party should recognise that under the agreement it may receive or become appraised of information belonging or relating to the other, including information concerning business and marketing plans, intellectual property, financial results, contractual arrangements, transactions etc.

Each party should agree

- Not to divulge confidential information belonging to the other to any third party (including a sub-contractor) except to the extent, and for the purposes, expressly anticipated in the agreement.
- Not to divulge confidential information belonging to the other to any of its employees who do not need to know it, without, in either case, the prior written consent of the other.

17.3 Personal data protection – the eighth principle

Privacy rights generally refer to an individual's right to control the distribution of his or her personal information. Privacy has long been an important issue in Europe, and it is becoming even more important with the use of the Internet and the ability to access and transfer personal data[152]. In contrast, privacy rights in Asia have historically been more relaxed than those in Europe[153].

Different countries have taken different approaches to privacy[154]. The European Union, for example, has long standing laws that strictly limit the processing and transfer of all personal information[155]. The United States has taken a more focused approach, limiting companies' ability to process data when that processing creates the possibility of real harm to individuals.

The Department of Constitutional Affairs in the UK is currently holding a consultation which proposes increasing penalties available to the courts to deter people who are guilty of trying to profit from the illegal trade in personal data or who deliberately supply personal data to those who have no right to see it.

When considering any type of data processing internal or by a service provider the company must consider what regulations apply to the processing in the jurisdiction where the data was collected. When data is transferred[156] to another jurisdiction for processing, such as in an offshore outsourcing relationship, the company

---

[152] Confidence and Data Protection, Privacy and Data Protection, PDP 4.8 (2), Sept 2004 by Peter Carey.

[153] India has not yet enacted a comprehensive data protection law.

[154] Privacy and Security Law Issues in Offshore Outsourcing Transactions, by Margaret. P. Eisenhauer.

[155] The EC Data Protection Directive recognises the European view that privacy is a fundamental human right, and establishes a general comprehensive legal framework that is aimed at protecting individuals and promoting individual choice regarding the processing of personal data. The Directive imposes an onerous set of requirements on any person that collects or processes data pertaining to individuals in their personal or professional capacity. It is based on a set of data protection principles, which include the legitimate basis, purpose limitation, data quality, proportionality, and transparency principles, data security and confidentiality, data subjects' rights of access, rectification, deletion and objection, restrictions on onwards transfers, additional protection where special categories of data and direct marketing are involved, and a prohibition on automated individual decisions. The Directive also regulates transfers of personal data. Subject to some limited exceptions, personal data may not be transferred to non-EC jurisdictions that do not offer an "adequate level of protection" for the data.

[156] The term "transfer" encompasses both actual (physical) movement of data to a processor located in another country as well as the remote access by the foreign processor to data held in the home jurisdiction. From a data protection law standpoint, the legal analysis does not change if the data itself travels or if it is merely accessed from a location in other jurisdiction.

must also consider how the laws (or lack of laws) in the target jurisdiction may affect the processing and its rights with respect to the information.

With regard to any trans-border data flow, each company must consider two separate legal perspectives:

- First, it must consider whether any laws in the country where the data originates will continue to regulate the data post-transfer.
- Second, it must consider whether laws in the country where the data is processed give rise to any additional risks or benefits.

The EU Data Protection Directive (95/46/EC) imposes obligations on the data controller rather than the data processor. This means that it is the customer in an outsourcing arrangement which must give careful consideration to compliance requirements.

According to the Data Protection Directive "personal data" is any information which relates to an identified or identifiable natural person. An identifiable person is one who can be identified, directly or indirectly, from the information – in particular by reference to an identification number or to one or more specific to an individual's physical, physiological, mental, economic, cultural or social identify. The breadth of this definition means that very few outsourcing transactions will not involve the processing of personal data. Further the Directive applies to the processing of personal data by automatic means (for example electronically held files) as well as to non-automatic processing, provided the non-automatic files form part of a structured filing system.

There is a further subset of personal data known as "sensitive personal data", which consists of special categories of data and is subject to additional safeguards. The scope of the directive is far reaching because of the wide definition of "processing", which includes obtaining, recording, storing, amending, retrieving, disclosing, and destroying the data.

The UK specifically introduced the Data Protection Act, 1998, which was informed by the EU Data Protection Directive. In many respects it is probably the most advanced in terms the application of Data protection principles as provided for within the EU framework and is therefore described in relatively high level of detail here.

The Act specifically imposes obligation on "data controllers", who are individuals or entities that determine the purpose for and the manner in which personal data will be processed. The role of the data controller is distinct from that of a data processor who merely processes data according to instructions of the data controller.

The Act requires "data controllers" to comply with the eight principles of the Act, namely that data must be:

1. Fairly and lawfully processed.
2. Processed for limited purposes.
3. Adequate, relevant and not excessive.
4. Accurate.
5. Not kept longer than necessary.
6. Processed in accordance with the data subject's rights.
7. Secure.
8. Not transferred to countries without "adequate" protection.

The eighth principle is principally derived from the requirements under the European Communities Directive 95/46/EC.

Most outsourcers legitimise the processing of personal data by stating that the "processing is necessary for the purpose of the legitimate interests pursued by the data controller balanced against the rights and freedoms of the data subject". On top of this legitimising requirement, the data controller has to ensure that the processing is also fair. The Fair Processing Code[157] helps in this respect, stating that the "data controller" must inform the data subject of the identity of the "data controller", the purpose of the processing and any other information needed to ensure fair processing.

Data processing may take place at several stages:

- During due diligence.
- Contract negotiation.
- Transition stage.
- Implementation.

At each stage, the customer will need to ensure that any transfer of personal data is undertaken on a fair and lawful basis.

Although compliance with all of the above Data Protection principles is necessary, the eighth principle takes on particular relevance in an offshore outsourcing arrangement. This principle states that: "Personal data shall not be transferred to a country or territory outside the European Economic Area unless that country or territory ensures an adequate level of protection for the rights and freedoms of data subjects in relation to the processing of personal data"[158].

---

[157] UK Data Protection Act 1998, at Schedule 1, Part II, paragraphs 1 to 4.

[158] Article 25 of the 1995 European Data Protection Directive requires that personal data may only be transferred to a third country that ensures an adequate level of protection. Third country is a term used by the Commission to describe any place outside the EEA.

In considering “adequacy”, the interpretative provisions of the Act relating to the eighth principle, state that consideration should be given to amongst other factors, the following:

1. The nature of the personal data.
2. The country or territory of origin of the information contained in the data.
3. The country or territory of final destination for that information.
4. The purposes for which, and period during which, the data is intended to be processed.
5. The law in force in the country or territory in question.
6. The international obligations of that country or territory.
7. Any relevant codes of conduct, or other rules, which are enforceable in that country or territory (whether generally or by arrangement in particular cases).
8. Any security measures taken in respect of the data in that country or territory.

In assessing adequacy, the UK “Information Commissioner”[159] recommends that the issue should be addressed by:

1. Considering whether (or the extent to which) the third country in question is the subject of a Community finding or presumption of adequacy.
2. Considering the type of transfer[160] involved, and whether this enables any presumption of adequacy or inadequacy.

---

[159] The Information Commissioner's Office is a UK independent supervisory authority, reporting directly to the UK Parliament and have an international role as well as a national one, and is supervised by European Data Protection Supervisor (EDPS). The EDPS is an independent supervisory authority devoted to protecting personal data and privacy and promoting good practice in the EU institutions and bodies. It does so by: monitoring the EU administration's processing of personal data; advising on policies and legislation that affect privacy; and co-operating with similar authorities to ensure consistent data protection.

[160] The Act does not define ‘transfer’ but the ordinary meaning of the word is transmission from one place, person, etc to another. Transfer does not mean the same as mere transit. Therefore the fact that the electronic transfer of personal data may be routed through a third country on its way from the UK to another EEA country does not bring such transfer within the scope of the Eighth Principle.
In the case of Bodil Lindqvist v Kammaraklagaren (2003) (Case C-101/01), the European Court of Justice held that *there was no transfer of personal data to a third country where an individual loaded personal data onto an internet page in a Member State using a internet hosting provider in that Member State, even though the page was accessible via the internet by people based in a third country. Instead, a transfer was only deemed to have taken place where the internet page was actually accessed by a person located in a third country. In practice, data are often loaded onto the internet with the intention that the data be accessed in a third country, and, as this will usually lead to a transfer, the principle in the Lindqvist case will not apply in such circumstances. However, in situations where there is no intention to transfer the data to a third country and no transfer is deemed to have taken place as the information has not been accessed in a*

3. Considering the factors referred to above, including the consideration of the application and use of contracts and/or codes of conduct to create adequacy.
4. Where there is no adequacy, or no complete certainty with regard to this, consideration should be given to the derogations contained in Schedule 4 of the UK Act, pursuant to which the transfer may proceed if any of those derogations are satisfied.

While a number of countries have been identified by the EU as having adequate data protection laws for the purposes of transfers of data to them (known as the "adequacy club")[161], India is not amongst them as yet.

17.3.1 Concept of legal adequacy

Where processing of sensitive data is going to be carried out abroad on an ongoing basis, a comprehensive investigation of the legal adequacy criteria will need to be carried out and an appropriate risk assessment completed.

If the general adequacy criteria reveal that the transfer is low risk, i.e. if it's a one off transfer and the personal data will be securely destroyed immediately afterwards, then it is unlikely to be necessary to carry out a review of the legal criteria.

When legal adequacy is assessed, an exporting controller should consider, in particular, the following questions:

- Has the country adopted the OECD Guidelines (Guidelines on the Protection of Privacy and Trans-border Flows of Personal Data' – Organisation for Economic Co-operation and Development, 1980) and, if so, what measures has it taken to implement them?
- Has the country ratified Convention 108 (Council of Europe Convention for the protection of individuals with regard to the automatic processing of personal data, Strasbourg 1981) and are there appropriate mechanisms in place for compliance with it?
- Does the country have a data protection regime in place which meets the standards set out in the Article 29 Working Party document adopted on 24 July

third country (i.e. the Eighth Principle does not apply), data controllers will still need to ensure that the processing complies with all of the other Principles. In particular, data controllers must consider the requirement in the First Data Protection Principle that the processing must be fair which may be contravened by making the data so widely accessible.

161 As of July 2006, the following countries outside of the EEA had been confirmed as adequate by the European Commission: Argentina, Canada, Guernsey, Isle of Man and Switzerland. In addition to findings relating to the above countries, the Commission has also made a finding regarding specific transfers to the United States of America by the use of Safe Harbor.

1998 (WP 12) (Transfers of personal data to third countries: Applying Articles 25 and 26 of the EU data protection directive'[162] - This sets out certain principles - such as the 'purpose limitation principle', the 'transparency principle' and the 'security principle' - which the Working Party believe should be embodied in a data protection regime in order for it to be considered to be adequate)?
- Does the third country have any legal framework for the protection of the rights and freedoms of individuals generally?
- Does the third country recognise the general rule of law and, in particular, the ability of parties to contract and bind themselves under contracts?
- More specifically, are there laws, rules or codes of practice (general or sectoral) which govern the processing of personal data?

The majority of outsource service providers seek to characterise their role as that of processor, rather than controller. This effectively limits their data protection compliance obligations to those specified in the contract. It is still common, to see contract terms simply requiring the parties to comply with their obligations under the Directive and relevant local laws. However the Directive does not impose any obligations on a mere data processor. An outsourcing customer could thus become unnecessarily exposed to risk as a result of their service provider's non compliant processing of personal data. It is better that companies specify in detail in the contract exactly what is required of the processor.

Where it is not possible to prove "adequacy", based on a risk assessment of all the general and legal criteria, then organisations seek to use the EC Directive's Model Clauses.

The EC has approved three sets of standard contractual clauses (known as model clauses) as providing adequate protection to transfer individual's personal information. Two sets of model clauses relate to transferring personal information from one company to another company who will use it for its own purposes. The other set is for transferring personal information to a processor acting under your instructions.

The Eighth Principle does not apply where the transfer has been made using any of the model clauses. This means that an exporting controller who uses these model clauses does not need to make a separate assessment of adequacy in relation to the transfer.

The use of Commission authorised standard contracts ('model clauses') or specific, approved binding corporate rules ('BCR') enable the transfer to be made exempt from the restrictions of the Eighth Principle on the basis that the model clauses or set of BCR provide adequate safeguards for the rights and freedoms of data subjects. This derives from Article 26(2)13 of the Directive which states that:

[162] Article 29 Working Party (DGXV D/5025/98 WP 12).

"a Member State may authorise a transfer or a set of transfers of personal data to a third country which does not ensure an adequate level of protection...where the controller adduces adequate safeguards with respect to the protection of the privacy and fundamental rights and freedoms of individuals and as regards the exercise of the corresponding rights; such safeguards may in particular result from appropriate contractual clauses..."

The model clauses contain obligations on both the data exporter and data importer to ensure that the transfer complies with the standards required by the Directive and the data subject has a right to directly enforce its rights under them. Under the Set I controller-controller model clauses, the data exporter and data importer are jointly and severally liable to the data subject for any damage it suffers as a result of a breach by either party of those of the model clauses under which the data subject is a beneficiary ('third party beneficiary clauses').

This differs from the Set II controller-controller model clauses under which the data subject can only enforce its rights against the party who is responsible for the relevant breach. Under the controller-processor model clauses, the data exporter is liable to the data subject for any breach by either party of the third party beneficiary clauses except in limited circumstances. However, if the breach was caused by the data importer, the data importer is required to indemnify the data exporter to the extent of its liability to the data subject.

None of the versions of the model clauses may be amended but the parties are free to include any other clauses on business related issues provided that they do not contradict the model clauses. Indeed, the Set II controller-controller model clauses include some suggested commercial clauses to be incorporated (e.g. an indemnity provision, dispute resolution clause and extra termination right).

The Eighth principle also provides for exemptions for the transfer of personal data. These exist to ensure it is possible to transfer data in exceptional situations, but their interpretation is very narrow – i.e. an exemption applies where it is necessary to protect the vital interests of the data subject – life and death situations. Organisations looking to outsource personal data for business purposes will rarely be able to apply any of the exemptions, expect where the data subject has consented to the transfer, although this may not legitimise the transfer.

17.3.2 Binding corporate rules (BCR)

BCRs are internal codes of conduct operating within a multinational organisation for the purposes of enabling transfer of data outside the EEA (but within the group) to be made on a basis which ensures adequate safeguards for the rights and freedoms of data subjects. They are designed to be a global solution for multinational companies by ensuring their intra-group transfers comply with the Eighth

Principle and providing a simple mechanism for obtaining the necessary authorisations across the EU.

Binding Corporate Rules may be relevant where the outsourcing model chosen is either the captive direct or a joint venture between the customer and a service provider.

17.3.3 Residual information

There is a common concern with respect to "residual information" – experience gained or information learned on the project (which could include the customer's confidential information). Service providers are wary of the potential adverse implications of such proscriptions on their ability to provide services to others in the future and as such, seek contractual provisions such as:

- *Not withstanding the confidentiality obligations of the service provider under this agreement, the service provider may during and after the term of this agreement use in its business any residual information. Residual information, for purposes of this agreement, means the ideas, know-how and techniques retained in the unaided memories of the service provider's personnel who have had access to the confidential information of the customer in the course of performing services under the outsourcing agreement.*

Customers generally object to such provisions. The customer needs to achieve an appropriate balance between allowing the natural honing of individual's skills during a project and protecting against acts designed to acquire from the customer its trade secrets and other intellectual property assets.

Residual information provisions at a minimum are intended to clarify the service provider's confidentiality obligations. The breadth and interpretation of the provision often depends on the parameters of the confidentiality provision.

Both service provider and customer should seek a compromise in establishing a balanced residual information provision. The supplier for instance could limit the provision to only information to which it has rightful access, whilst the customer could identify particular categories of sensitive information that should be held strictly confidential, while permitting a less stringent treatment of other customer confidential information.

Customers and service providers typically find it difficult to reach an agreement on the definition of "unaided memory". A typical definition is "information the employee has not retained a copy of the information and has not intentionally memorized the information, other than to perform the outsourced services".

17.4 Data transfer in the interests of the data subject

There is a list of exemptions to the ban on the export of personal data outside the EEA (under the eighth Data Protection Principle). These exemptions are set out in Schedule 4 to the UK Data Protection Act[163]. Consent of the data subject to the transfer is just one of the exemptions. Authorisation from the Information Commissioner that the transfer has been made in such a manner as to ensure adequate safeguards for the data subjects, through use of the Information Commissioner's model contract is another. Article 2(h) of the Directive defines consent as "any freely given specific and informed indication of [the data subject's] wishes by which the data subject signifies his agreement to personal data relating to him being processed".

Consequently, exporting controllers should be able to produce clear evidence of the data subject's consent in any particular case and may be required to demonstrate that the data subject was informed as required. Similarly, valid consent means that the data subject must have a real opportunity to withhold their consent without suffering any penalty, or to withdraw it subsequently if they change their mind. This can be particularly relevant if it is employee consent which is being sought. For these reasons, consent is unlikely to provide an adequate long-term framework for data controllers in cases of repeated or structural transfers of data to a third country. As Article 29 Working Party states in its paper on the interpretation of Article 26(1): "relying on consent may…prove to be a 'false good solution', simple at first glance but in reality complex and cumbersome"[164].

In order to send data overseas it needs to be shown that the transfer is necessary for the performance of entering into the contract. If it is a third party entering into the contract, rather than the data subject, then it has to be clearly shown that they are entering into it at the request of the data subject or that it is clearly in the data subject's interests.

An example given by Article 29 of the Working Party for a contract that falls within this category is where there is a transfer to a third country by travel agents of personal data of their clients to hotels or to other commercial partners that will organise the clients' stay. This is contrasted with the transfer of employee data from an EEA subsidiary to a non-EEA parent company in order to centralise a multinational group's HR and payment functions which, it has been argued, is necessary for the data subject's employment contract with the data controller. Although such a transfer may provide a cost efficiency which may indirectly benefit the employee, it would be difficult to show that the centralisation of payment functions is objectively necessary for the performance of the data subject's em-

---

[163] Data Protection Act, 1998.

[164] Article 29 Working Party's Working document on a common interpretation of Article 26(1) of Directive 95/46/EC (2093/05/EN – WP114) page 11.

ployment contract and could not be carried out elsewhere. Therefore it is likely that in these circumstances the derogation would not apply.

Similarly, where the contract is between the data controller and a third party, not only does the data controller need to show that the transfer is necessary for that contract, unless the contract has been entered into at the data subject's request, the data controller needs to show "a close and substantial connection between the data subject's interests and the purpose of the contract".

It is sometimes argued by data controllers that a transfer which is necessary for an outsourcing contract with a service provider in a third country will fall under this derogation where the subject of the contract is indirectly in the interests of the data subjects.

However, the Commissioner[165] does not usually support such a view on the basis that there is not a sufficiently close and substantial link between the contract and the data subject's interests. Instead the Commissioner would, as a general rule, expect such arrangements to comply with, or be exempt from, the Eighth Principle through other means – such as the adducing of adequacy or the implementation of adequate safeguards.

The Information Commissioner's Office (ICO) issued its first enforcement notice against the operators of a website (www.b4usearch.com) for breach of data protection legislation, and has warned that it will actively investigate other organisations undertaking similar breaches. The website offered a free people search facility and had used personal data collated from electoral registers published before 2002, when the law change to allow individuals to opt-out of the version of the electoral register that is sold to third parties. Therefore the website had not processed the data fairly or lawfully, as it did not have the data subjects' permission to use that data.

17.5 The Seventh Principle

Where there is a transfer to a data processor, wherever that processor is located, a data controller must comply with the requirements of the Seventh Data Protection Principle (the 'Seventh Principle') which states that: "Appropriate technical and organisational measures shall be taken against unauthorised or unlawful processing of personal data and against accidental loss or destruction of, or damage to, personal data".

[165] In common with the Article 29 Working Party (See pages 13-14 of WP 114).

The Seventh Principle[166] requires that where a third party undertakes processing on behalf of a data controller, that data controller must:

- (a) choose a data processor providing sufficient guarantees in respect of the technical and organisational security measures governing the processing to be carried out.
- (b) take reasonable steps to ensure compliance with those measures (such as conducting regular audits and reviews). In addition, a data controller will not be regarded as complying with the Seventh Principle unless the processing is carried out under a contract "made or evidenced in writing"[167] and under which the data processor is to act only on instructions from the data controller and which contains an obligation on the part of the data processor to comply with provisions equivalent to those imposed on a data controller by the Seventh Principle.

Many outsourcing customers impose security obligations on service providers covering such things as security measures relating to the systems over which data may be transferred, accessed, manipulated and stored, organisational security measures governing access to premises and prohibition on staff bringing data storage devices on the premises (memory stick, CDs, mobile phones, cameras etc).

In addition customers should undertake due diligence on aspects of data security. Key issues to consider include:

- Keep confidential all information provided by the customer, on behalf of the customer, or as a result of performing services for the customer.
- Abide by all relevant privacy laws including those listed in the agreement.
- Allow security audits on the service provider's systems, including hiring an ethical hacking firm to test the strength of the service provider's firewalls.
- Protect all information whether or not confidential with appropriate physical and logical controls.
- Revoke access for any user upon a security breach or customer request.
- Use reasonable efforts, including employment of industry standard virus protection software, to avoid viruses, worms, back doors, trap doors, time bombs and other malicious software.
- Provide a copy of all customer data in the service provider's possession or under its control, in a reasonable format, upon customer's request.
- Never grant any subcontractor access to the service provider's data unless the service provider has approved the subcontractor and the subcontract includes all of the security provisions of the outsourced agreement.
- Report all security breaches or incidents to the customer.
- Have, maintain and follow an acceptable business recovery plan.

---

166 At paragraph 11 of Part II of Schedule 1 to the Act.

167 Schedule 1, Part II, paragraph 12(a)(i).

Customers should ensure they undertake regular audits of the service provider and ensure that audit rights are part of the contract. The Information Commissioner (ICO) refers to ISO27001 (previously BS 7799), the international standard for Information Security Management Systems (ISMS) as a suitable means to ensure appropriate technical and organizational measures are in place to safeguard personal data.

Use of model clauses and assessment of adequacy

One form that such a contract "made or evidenced in writing" may take is the data controller-data processor model clauses discussed above which have been approved by the Commission as offering adequate safeguards for the purposes of Article 26(2)[168].

The use of these terms can simultaneously satisfy the requirement for a contract in the Seventh Principle and fall under a derogation from the Eighth Principle and, for that reason, may be attractive in data controller-data processor international outsourcings.

However, a data controller within Europe need not necessarily use these controller-processor model clauses when entering into a contract with a data processor in a third country provided that any contractual arrangement satisfies the requirements of the Seventh Principle and the data controller has successfully complied with, or derogated from, the Eighth Principle by another means. The model clauses are merely one method of addressing the requirements of the Eighth Principle.

In particular, the model clauses will not be necessary if the data controller establishes that there is adequacy. In this respect, the Commissioner's guidance is that compliance with the Seventh Principle will go some way towards satisfying the adequacy requirements of the Eighth Principle (given the continuing contractual relationship between the parties and the data controller's continued liability for data protection compliance under the Act). However, the Commissioner would still expect the data controller to make due diligence checks in relation to the data processor and conduct some examination of the type of matters usually looked at in relation to adequacy (e.g. the nature of the data, the country in which the data processor is located and the security arrangements in that third country).

17.6 The situation in India with respect to data protection

Many customers or prospective customers have legitimate concerns that India does not have the same stringent standards of protection of personal data that are

168 Commission Decision 2002/16/EC (dated 27 December 2001).

required by the EU Data Protection Act. The Indian Government has taken steps to introduce data protection legislation in a bid to ensure that European and US companies looking to outsource services overseas will consider India as their optimal choice. The proposed legislation is intended to implement a data protection regime of a standard acceptable to the US and the EU[169]. However, as it currently stands, the legislation is far from the EU model.

The Indian government has enacted a comprehensive set of electronic commerce regulations, the Information Technology Act 2000[170]. This Act addresses computer crimes, including hacking, damage to computer source code, and breach of confidentiality provisions. The Act also created a Cyber Appellate Tribunal to handle cyber crime cases.

17.6.1 Current legislation governing data privacy in India

Indian courts have interpreted the right of privacy as an unarticulated fundamental right against an action by the state. There are a number of different legislation that effect data privacy in India, these include:

- The Indian Contract Act of 1872 – This defines the legal framework for writing and honouring contracts.
- The Information Technology Act of 2000 – Creates legal recognition of electronic records and communications. Also lists various types of cyber crimes, calling for the appointment of special adjudicating officers for cyber crimes, the establishment of a Cyber Appellate Tribunal, as well as an Advisory Committee. However it remains silent on the issues of privacy, protection and regulated use of data. The Act only covers unauthorised access and data theft from computer and networks. Also worth noting is that the Act addresses the issue of privacy rights, however this is quite narrow, with the Act only protecting privacy rights from government action.
- Arbitration and Conciliation Act of 1996 – this outlines the process for setting an arbitration agreement in a contract, and how to initiate an arbitration hearing. It is valuable because privacy tends to be set in contracts and courts can take years to adjudicate disputes.
- The Specific Relief Act of 1963 – Offers an avenue for legal restitution when performance of an activity described in a contract is difficult to ascertain, or

---

[169] India at the Crossroads; Privacy and Security Law in India, IAPP Privacy and Data Security Academy and Expo, by Richard. M Rossow.

[170] The Act came into force on 17th October 2000. This Act although modelled on UNCITRAL's Model Law, departs in many respects from the spirit of the model law. Furthermore, the Indian courts have not yet found any opportunity to appraise the impact of the provisions of the Act on substantial principles of contract formation codified in the Indian Contract Act 1872.

when monetary compensation for non-performance of the contracted activity will not afford adequate relief.

- The Indian Penal Code of 1960 – Outlines basic descriptions of crime and punishment.
- The Consumer Protection Act of 1986 – Sets up a national, state and local consumer protection board where consumers and consumer groups can seek redress against companies, which may allow redress for privacy issues.
- The India Copyright Act (discussed in later chapter).

In practice, many companies hiring employees include confidentiality and privacy as part of their contract. Hence for any breach the employee is liable under the IT Act, Indian Contract Act and the Indian Penal Code. The Information Technology Act 2000 provides some protection regarding data and proprietary rights. Tough penalties (including imprisonment) are provided for offences including:

- Unlawfully accessing computer networks.
- Unlawfully downloading copies.
- Tampering with electronic files.
- Computer hacking.
- Disclosing confidential information without authorisation.

However, India does not appear to want to rush into drafting and adopting data privacy laws, possibly due to the fact that there is not a history embedded with abuses of privacy, and that there doesn't appear to be a problem of identity theft in India.

To reduce the risks of misuse of non-public personal data, some service provider companies in India also have adopted one or more of the following stringent security measures[171]:

- Armed guards are posted outside offices.
- Entry is restricted by requiring microchip-embedded swipe cards.
- Bags and briefcases are prohibited in the work area.
- Computers in workstations have no printers or devices for removable storage.
- Agents /visitors are banned from carrying mobile phones to the production floor.
- Phone calls to and from either family or friends are forbidden in employee workstations.
- Image capturing devices like cell phones, scanners or photocopiers are not allowed.

---

171 Offshore Outsourcing to India by US and EU companies: Legal and cross-cultural issues that affect data privacy regulation in BPO, by Barbara Crutchfield George and Deborah Roach Gaut 6 U.C. Davis Bus L.J. 13 (2006).

- Internet and email access are prohibited at workstations and inside most BPO companies.
- Key information, such as passwords that clients provide is encrypted and thus is unseen by employees.
- Employees are monitored via closed circuit TV.

Business corruption is also perceived as a problem in India according to the latest figures from Transparency International[172]. This only adds to the perception that data and sensitive information will not be entirely safe when transferring data to an Indian service provider.

Without a strong legal framework which can offer protection, it becomes more important that the contract is specific and imposes obligations upon the service provider for such data protection.

However, customers should put such risks into perspective – the amount of effort individual outsourcing service providers invest with elaborate security systems and employee vetting is unmatched in many developed countries from where the customer usually originates. It would seem the probability of misuse of personnel data can be equally applicable to a transfer of data within a European country or a transfer of data to an Indian service provider.

The next chapter discusses the issues that are relevant in respect of protecting IPR for companies outsourcing to India.

[172] Ibid.

18. Intellectual property rights (IPR)

This chapter discusses the issues that are relevant in respect of protecting IPR for companies outsourcing to India.

18.1 Intellectual property rights is an integral part of the outsourcing agreement

Use and ownership of intellectual property are key issues in the outsourcing agreements because the outsourcing relationship, depending on the nature of the services, often produces new or improved products, services, technologies or other intellectual property.

The outsourcing agreement should state whether the customer or the service provider will retain ownership of any intellectual property that may be used or developed by the other party during the course of their arrangement. The agreement should also address the issue of which party will own the results of any new developments or improvements.

In order to provide an outsourced service, it is often necessary for the service provider to use existing third party IPR which is licensed or provided under contract to the customer. Under such circumstances, it is essential that the customer obtains the necessary authorisation from the third party owner of the IPR before the service provider has access to the IPR.

In some instances it may be preferable for the IPR to be assigned or novated to the service provider so that he can take control of all the IPR which is needed to deliver the service. Such assignment is usually executed on the basis that the service provider's additional rights will exist for the duration of the outsourcing contract, but will pass back to the customer or be transferred to the incoming 3rd party outsourcer when the contract is terminated or expires.

The ability to re-deploy solutions by service providers more easily for other customers raises new issues. The customer may want to share in the revenue from such re-deployment. In addition the customer will naturally object to providing the solution to third parties it perceives as competitors. The parties should address these issues beforehand in their agreement. In addition the customer will not want a blanket grant of IP rights to the service provider, at least not if it carefully considers the implications of patent rights. Patents cover entire processes, methods and inventions. Thus if a service provider secures a patent in inventions that it discovers in the course of providing services to the customer, it could block the customer from using or improving inventions crucial to its business. The patent problem is particularly acute for the customer where development occurs in the context of outsourcing, as the service provider may become deeply involved in a portion of the customer's business. Development and customisation make the customer more vulnerable to the service provider with respect to updates, renewal pricing and termination.

Intellectual property rights are essentially territorial in nature so, where registration is necessary, for patents, registered designs and trade marks, these will not exist in other countries unless registration has been sought and obtained there[173].

Europe has well developed laws regarding patents, trademarks and copyrights, and almost all of the European countries are members of key treaties, such as the Berne Convention and the Madrid Protocol, which help to standardize the level of protection afforded to copyrights and trademarks[174] [175].

Patents only give protection in the country where they are registered. Where wider protection is required, there are a number of choices:

- The European Patent Convention (EPC) – established a singe process run by the European Patent Office (EPO). The application and grants are centralised but infringement actions must be taken in each relevant state.
- The Community Patent - plans for a single European Community patent have been around for some time – soon to be implemented, the system will allow the grant of one patent valid throughout the community.

---

173 UK patent Office.

174 UK is a member of the following WIP treaties: Paris convention, Berne Convention, Madrid Protocol.

175 On 6th July 2005 the European Parliament rejected the draft Directive on patentability of computer implemented inventions ("the Software Directive"). This means the end for the Software Directive which was introduced to harmonize software patenting throughout Europe. While the Member State's laws and European Patent Convention prohibit the patenting of software programs, the law is unclear due to the inconsistency of approach by the different Member States. The purpose for harmonizing the law in this area was to ensure that truly innovative inventions that contribute to technology and lead to advancements within the field are protected, not the software itself. The situation now is that patents for computerized inventions will continue to be granted but in an environment where there is a disparity of approach by the various National Patent Offices. Accordingly, in the event of a patent being granted for software by a National Patent Office, the burden will now rest on third parties to object to the Patent.

- The Patent Co-operation Treaty (PCT) – Under this treaty, which is wider than the EPC, initial application is made centrally before grant in separate states. The PCT is administered by the World Intellectual Property Organisation (WIPO)[176].

In contrast to the laws in Europe, the enforcement of laws protecting copyrights and trademarks in Asian countries is relatively new and continues to develop. Accordingly, a substantial amount of commercial software developed in these countries remains subject to piracy[177].

Under law, absent contrary agreement, the service provider will own developments it creates. The service provider typically wants to retain ownership of IP in order to resell / reuse the IP. The customer however does not want to pay for solutions that end up being used by competitors. Business process patents make the problem even more pronounced. Use of open source software may complicate IP issues (e.g., customer access to source code may survive outsourcing relationship).

The International Intellectual Property Alliance (IIPA) reports that "corporate end user piracy is endemic in major Indian companies"[178]. Despite the reported high level of wilful copyright infringement in business settings, since enactment of India's 1995 copyright law, "there have been no criminal convictions for software piracy"[179]. One possible explanation, according to IIPA, is that criminal copyright cases in India "can take 12 years to complete". Civil cases are also reportedly "long" and "drawn-out" because of an under-resourced and bureaucratic judicial system[180]. IIPA has stated that amendments to India's Copyright Act implemented in 1995, "result(ed) in one of the most modern copyright laws in any country"[181]

---

[176] 1883 marked the birth of the Paris Convention for the Protection of Industrial Property, the first major international treaty designed to help the people of one country obtain protection in other countries for their intellectual creations. The Paris Convention entered into force in 1884 with 14 member States. In 1886, copyright entered the international arena with the Berne Convention for the Protection of Literary and Artistic Works. Like the Paris Convention, the Berne Convention set up an International Bureau to carry out administrative tasks. In 1974, WIPO became a specialized agency of the United Nations system of organizations, with a mandate to administer intellectual property matters recognized by the member States of the UN. WIPO expanded its role and further demonstrated the importance of intellectual property rights in the management of globalised trade in 1996 by entering into a cooperation agreement with the World Trade Organization (WTO).

[177] International Intellectual Property Alliance, "India" in 2002 Special 301 Report on Global Copyright Protection and Enforcement 128 (App. C).

[178] Ibid.

[179] Ibid.

[180] Ibid.

[181] International Intellectual Property Alliance, supra n.11 at 138.

With this backdrop of privacy, where enforcement of legal rights is both a bureaucratic and a time consuming process, customers must ensure an IP due diligence enquiry is undertaken before finalising any outsourcing plan to safeguard a company's IP before outsourcing to India. Undertaking an IP due diligence can be quite a lengthy process for larger customers considering outsourcing their services.

An IP Due-Diligence enquiry check-list should:

- Identify internally and document IP: trade secrets, trademarks, patents, industrial designs, copyright and related rights.
- Identify internally the inventor, creator or author of the IP.
- Determine ownership rights in the identified IP.
- Identify contracts or other agreements associated with the IP, e.g. technology transfer or licensing agreements; confidentiality and non-compete agreements.
- Identify assigned or licensed IP used by the service provider: IP of third parties and or by employees.
- Identify existing and or alleged breaches of contract, infringements, disclosures of confidential information and trade secrets for the service provider.
- Determine jurisdiction and enforcement: applicable laws, enforceability, and expressly assign IP rights from the employee of a service provider to the customer, if appropriate.

In many cases, agreements fail to specify in concrete terms which laws governs the agreement, many fail to state the country or indeed state (especially with respect to the USA) as the sole and exclusive jurisdiction. Failure to state the specific jurisdiction can lead to problems should litigation be necessary. As an example, Israeli law specifies that all cases involving Israeli companies must be tried in Israel unless the contract specifies the sole and exclusive jurisdiction elsewhere.

Outsourcing customers should have some comfort in that India has signed the Berne convention. The body of law governs intellectual property; its participants agree to recognize the existence and the ownership of intellectual property and not use it in an unauthorized manner. In addition Indian courts appear to take infringement more seriously now and in a number of cases have awarded injunctions and fines[182].

---

182 In Microsoft Corporation v Mr Yogesh Papat & Anr 118 (2205) DLT580 where the defendants without a license loaded Microsoft software in the computers they were selling, the court granted permanent injunction and awarded Microsoft Rs 19.75 lacs. In CIASCO Technologies v. Shrkanth MANU/DE/2809/2005 the court granted an injunction and under that no consignment other than that belonging to the plaintiff bearing the "CISCO" trademark could be permitted to enter the country.

18.2 Copyright

India has one of the most modern copyright laws in any country[183]. Despite the statutory regime, enforcement is considered lax and violations of the law such as software privacy are widespread.

India's Copyright Act protects computer programs, among other "works of authorship". In keeping with international copyright principles, the Indian Copyright Act provides that the copyright in an original book, including any "derivative work", will be owned by the individual who created it. This individual will enjoy the "economic rights" in the work, in addition to "moral rights", such as the right to attribution. The Copyright Act recognizes the concept of "work for hire", accordingly when an employee creates a work in the scope of his employment, the employer will normally be deemed to own the "economic rights" in the work. However the employee will generally retain the "moral rights".

The customer should also ensure the outsourcing arrangement is sufficient in terms of assigning to it, such rights in the computer programs and other works of authorship that the Indian service provider may create. This concern is especially relevant where the service provider performs the development work through independent contractors or third party sub-contractors. The outsourcing arrangement should also seek to deal with the issue of inalienable "moral rights". The risk of an author asserting moral rights can be minimised if the assignment agreement with the author contains an irrevocable waiver and agreement to never assert moral rights. This should be included in each employee's invention assignment agreement and in agreements with consultants.

In addition, when determining the nature of the rights to be assigned back to the customer, the customer should be cognisant of the fact that it will generally not have standing to sue for infringement or recover lost profits absent a transfer of full legal title or an exclusive license under the relevant copyright.

18.3 The Indian Copyright Act

Section 18 of the Copyright Act of India provides that the owner of the copyright in an existing work or the prospective owner of the copyright in the future work may assign the copyright either wholly or partially and either generally or subject to limitations and either for the whole term of the copyright or any part thereof.

183 According to the International Intellectual Property Alliance and survey conducted by NASSCOM-Evalueserve study, in July 2004 called "Indian Information Security".

Section 19 of the Act, however, imposes important additional requirements for valid copyright assignments. In addition to being signed and in writing, under section 18(1), assignments must meet the following requirements, under section 18(2) through to Section 18(6):

- (2) The assignment of copyright in any work shall identify such work and shall specify the rights assigned and the duration and territorial extent of such assignment
- (3) The assignment of copyright in any work shall also specify the amount of royalty payable, if any, to the author or his legal heirs during the currency of the assignment and the assignment shall be subject to revision, extension or termination on terms mutually agreed upon by the parties.
- (4) Where the assignee does not exercise the rights assigned to him under any of the other sub-sections of this section within a period of one year from the date of assignment, the assignment in respect of such rights shall be deemed to have lapsed after the expiry of the said period unless otherwise specified in the assignment.
- (5) If the period of assignment is not stated, it shall be deemed to be five years from the date of assignment.
- (6) If the territorial extent of assignment is not specified, it shall be presumed to extend within India.

The Act leaves unclear whether and to what extent these provisions have any effect on contracts that expressly assign or license the entire copyright generally (i.e. no limitation of term or territory is to apply to the assignment).

India's Copyright Act[184] was recently amended to create new "fair use" rights for software that seems to go far beyond fair use rights under European Law for instance; thus an outsourcing customer that provides proprietary software may seek to narrow the license granted to the service provider to strictly limit uses of the software, than otherwise would be permissible under Indian law.

India has signed many international treaties which oblige it to observe agreed principles in Law.

[184] The Copyright (Amendment) Act, 1999 (India).

India's Treaty obligations include:

Treaty	Status	Entry into Force
• Berne Convention	• In Force	• April 1928
• Budapest Treaty	• In Force	• Dec 2001
• Film Register Treaty	• Signature	•
• Nairobi Treaty	• In Force	• Oct 1983
• Paris Convention	• In Force	• Dec 1998
• PCT	• In Force	• Dec 1998
• Phonograms Convention	• In Force	• Feb 1975
• Rome Convention	• Signature	•
• Washington Treaty	• Signature	•
• WIPO Convention	• In Force	• May 1975

Fig.8. India's Treaty Obligation – source: WIPO

18.4 Trade Marks

India has amended its Trade Mark Law in 1999 by widening the definition of trade mark by including both goods and services. The law relating to Industrial Design has been amended in 2000.

The law relating to Copyright is already at par with acceptable International standard, for India is a member of both the Bern Convention and Universal Copyright Convention (UCC).

The Trade Marks Act 1999 and the Trade Marks Rules 2002 came into force with effect from 15th September 2003. The Act enlarges the definition of "Mark" and "Trademark". It also provides for Registration of "Collective Marks" and "Service Marks" in addition to goods. Article 15 to 18 of TRIPS[185] provides that term of registration should not be for less than 7 years. In the Indian Act of 1999 the term of Registration is for 10 years and for renewal it is for a term of 10 years.

The Trademark Act of 1999 states the use of trademark for export trade, whether it be in respect of goods or in relation to services for use outside India is deemed to be use of trademark or service mark in India for any purpose for which such use is material under the Trade Marks Act 1999.

185 The WTO's Agreement on Trade-Related Aspects of Intellectual Property Rights (TRIPS), negotiated in the 1986-94 Uruguay Round introduced intellectual property rules into the multilateral trading system for the first time.

There is no specific Indian legislation for statutory protection of trade secrets or confidential information. Several precedents from Indian Courts have been made which provide for specifically enforcing confidentially agreements through mandatory injunctions. Confidential Information or trade secrets are protected as between the disclosing party and the recipient[186].

18.4.1 Comparative analysis of patent, copyright and trademark

	PATENT	COPYRIGHT	TRADEMARK
Right Protected	Right conferred in respect of a new invention to manufacture the product patented or use the process patented.	Right conferred in respect of original, literary, dramatic, musical and artistic works, cinematograph film and records.	Right conferred to use a particular mark, which may be a symbol, word, device applied to articles of commerce to indicate the distinctiveness of goods.
Time Period	14 years and in case of food and drugs 5 or 7 years.	Life time plus 50 years for literary, dramatic, musical and artistic works. 50 years from year of publication for records.	10 years and may be renewed from time to time.
Who Can Register	Actual inventor or an assignee of the right to make an application or legal representative of either.	The author or publisher of, or owner of or other person interested in the copyright in any work.	Proprietor of the trademark and application may be made in the name of an individual, partners of a Firm, Corporation, Government department or Trust.
Commercial Use	Assigning rights or licensing them to industrialists for a lump sum payment or royalty basis.	By assigning or licensing the right to others on a royalty or lump sum basis.	Licensing the right by registration of the licensee as a registered user.
Remedy For Infringement	Injunction, Damages, Accounts of profits.	Civil, Criminal, Administrative.	Injunction, Damages, Accounts of profits

Fig.9. Comparative analysis of patent, copyright, copyright and trademark: adapted from information from D Sagar and Associates: Advocates and Solicitors

[186] Through standard Non Disclosure Agreements (NDAs).

18.4.2 Domain names

Indian legislation protects only trademarks, and trademarks are associated with goods. Since domain names are not associated with goods, but rather with locations on the internet, they are not protected under trademark legislation. However, courts have involved the common law concept of "passing off" when settling disputes involving domain names[187]. Until such time as domain names are statutorily protected, courts may have to rely on common law principles to determine domain name disputes.

18.4.3 E-Commerce

E-commerce includes the whole gambit of commercial activities taking place in the cyber medium. The fundamentals of E-commerce rest mainly on the legality of E-contracts entered into between two or more parties apart from other civil and criminal aspects. In India, as elsewhere, currently cyber law is an undefined area of law – on offshoot of commercial law – without precedent, pronounced judgements and case law. The Information Technology Act 2000 attempts to address this area and covers such matters as Digital Signatures, electronic governance, transactions of electronic records etc. However, it is yet to be tested in force.

The next chapter discusses the important area of employee rights under outsourcing arrangements. This is largely driven by the EU Directive which provides extensive levels of protection for employees that are transferred as a result of outsourcing. This is clearly important as many customers outsource with the intention of reducing their employee costs and commitments – this may be tempered with by the impact of the EU Directive.

[187] Yahoo!Inc. v. Akash Arora &Anr. IPLR 1999 April 196 (Delhi HC).

19. Transferring employees as part of the outsourcing agreement

Many outsourcing agreements are typically predicated on cost savings, usually achieved by transferring work and sometime the staff who undertake such work to an outsourcing service provider. In EU countries, legislation provides certain rights to those employees being transferred. This chapter discusses the implications for companies who may be considering transferring staff to the outsourcing service provider.

19.1 Concept of Acquired Rights

In EU countries, legislation enacted under the European Commission's Acquired Right Directive[188] generally provides that transferred employees be given the same or comparable employment terms and benefits (including severance packages) as provided by the former employer.

The Transfer of Undertakings (Protection of Employment) Regulations 1981 and 2006 which are known as TUPE in the UK implements the European Community Acquired Rights Directive.

Outsourcing activity inevitably has staffing implications. The introduction of the amendment of the Acquired Rights Directive in June 1998 changed TUPE[189] and contained a new, more explicit definition of a "transfer of an undertaking".

Where a business changes hands, then at common law the contract may either be terminated or it may become frustrated, particularly where this follows the owner's insolvency, and under Statute there would generally be a redundancy situation. However, the Directive requires and the TUPE has the effect that the contract of employment can continue between the employee and the new owner.

The regulations apply where there is a "relevant transfer", which is described in Regulation 3 as "being a transfer of an undertaking or a part of one situated im-

---

[188] The Regulations were introduced to implement the Acquired Rights Directive (Directive 77/187), now replaced by Directive 2001/23.

[189] Transfer of Undertakings (Protection of Employment) Regulations 1981 (TUPE).

mediately before the transfer in the Home country. Regulation 2 defines an "undertaking" to include any trade or business".

European cases on the meaning of a "relevant transfer" have followed constantly from Spijkers v Gebroders Benedik Abbattoir CV[190], which laid down general principles and the decision in Dr. Sophie Redmond Stichting v Barton[191] led to the regulations being amended so that their operation was not confined to commercial ventures.

The extent of the meaning of "economic entity" was also discussed by the Employment Appeals Tribunal in Wynnwith Engineering Co. Ltd. v Bennett[192].

19.2 When does the Acquired Rights Directive and TUPE apply to outsourcing?

The regulations can apply regardless of the size of the transferred undertaking. The Regulations equally apply to transfer of a large business with many thousands of employees to very small companies.

For several years, TUPE was understood as applying principally to the sale of a trade or business, or part of a business, to a new owner - the distinction being between the transfer of a business as a going concern and a mere transfer of assets. Ayse Suzen v Zehnacker Gebaudereinigung GmbH Krankenhausservice[193] altered this developed view to one where the decisive question in identifying a transfer of an undertaking is whether the entity retains its identity after the transfer. The European Court of Justice (ECJ) held that the Acquired Rights Directive would only apply if:

- There was a transfer of tangible or intangible assets.
- The second contractor employed a substantial part of the employees formerly assigned by the first contractor to the activity.

In Rygaard v Stro Molle Akustik[194], it was held that short-term contracts were not covered - to be "an undertaking" the function had to be "stable". Ayse Suzen v Zehnacker Gebaudereinigung GmbH Krankenhausservice was embraced by UK courts and tribunals[195]. The result was that where no assets could practically trans-

---

190 Spijkers v Gebroders Benedik Abbattoir CV [1986] IRLR 2.
191 Dr. Sophie Redmond Stichting v Barton [1992] IRLR 366.
192 Wynnwith Engineering Co. Ltd. v Bennett [2002] IRLR 170.
193 Ayse Suzen v Zehnacker Gebaudereinigung GmbH Krankenhausservice (C13/95) [1997] All E.R. (EC) 289 (ECJ).
194 Rygaard v Stro Molle Akustik ASC - 48/94 [1996] IRLR 51 ECJ.
195 Betts v Brintel Helicopters Ltd 1997 IRLR 362 (CA).

fer, the incoming contractor could effectively control the application or otherwise of TUPE by deciding which of the transferor's employees to retain.

Where an economic entity is labour intensive, the existence of a TUPE transfer will depend on whether or not the workforce was taken on. A transfer will be found to take place where the principal reason for not taking the workforce on was to avoid the application of TUPE.

19.3 Asset based activities

The later ECJ decision: Oy Liikenne Ab v Liskojarvi and another[196] stated that the absence of any significant transfer of assets was decisive - "the tangible assets contribute significantly to the performance of the activity". Accordingly, a transfer of significant assets is essential for there to be an economic entity that retained its identity.

There can only be a transfer of a "people-orientated" activity if a significant transfer of staff takes place. In contrast, in an "asset-orientated" activity, there must be a significant transfer of tangible assets for TUPE to apply, regardless of the number of employees that go across.

19.4 Employment transfers[197]

Where there is a transfer of an "undertaking", TUPE provides that the employees' employment contracts pass to the new employer, provided:

1. They are employees - be they part-time, temporary, employees on maternity leave or sick leave, but not self-employed or agency workers.
2. They are employed by transferor - TUPE may not cover secondees.
3. Their employment would otherwise terminate - TUPE only applies to contracts that would "otherwise have terminated by the transfer".
4. They are assigned to the undertaking or part being transferred.
5. They do not object - employees have a right to be informed of the transfer and to object to being transferred; if the employee raises no objection, there is deemed no dismissal and neither the transferor nor the transferee is liable to the employee. There is no formal procedure for objecting - but it is necessary to distinguish between a true objection (i.e. a refusal) and a mere protest. If an employee resigns in advance of a TUPE transfer because of significantly

[196] Oy Liikenne Ab v Liskojarvi (Case 172/99) ECJ 25 January 2001.

[197] Transfer of Undertaking (protection of employment) Regulations 1981, UK Government proposals by DTI, June 2005.

worse terms and conditions on offer from the transferee, he/she can claim to have been constructively and unfairly dismissed by the transferor.

19.5 What obligations and rights pass to the transferor?

All rights and obligations under the employment contract (including future claims, e.g. accrued holiday rights, unpaid bonus or commission, and trade union recognition) transfer to the transferee. The employees' past employment counts as continuous, though now with the transferee. One area which is still somewhat unclear is pensions. Both TUPE and the Acquired Rights Directive currently exclude pension rights as they relate to rights to old age or retirement benefits under occupational pension schemes.

With effect from 6 April 2005 section 257 and 258 of the UK Pensions Act 2004, introduced a new minimum level of protection to the transferring employee rights in relation to pensions. Membership of occupational pension schemes as a stakeholder arrangement must be offered as a contractual condition by the transferee. The transferred employee can waive the protection afforded by section 258(6), but only in relation to those rights not arising from an EU Acquired Rights Directive.

19.6 Negotiating the contract in respect of transfer of employees

It is obviously essential for the customer and service provider to learn as much as possible about the terms and conditions of the employees and the potential liabilities which arise from the agreement, such as accrued holiday and wages up to the day of completion.

The following are commonly requested:

1. Warranties by the service provider that the information supplied is accurate and comprehensive, that no employees other than those listed will transfer, and that all necessary information to enable the transferee to comply with their respective information and consultation obligations has been supplied.
2. Indemnities sought by the customer may include indemnities in respect of claims brought by the transferring employee which arises out of the transfer. The service provider may also seek indemnities in respect of claims that had their source or origin before the transfer (e.g. dismissals, unpaid salary, discrimination claims), by employees not transferring, and indemnities arising out of the Acquired Rights Directive (or TUPE) if the parties have concluded that neither apply.

Customers in turn must monitor the service provider's activities. It is common to restrict the changing of staff or terms and conditions, and it is undesirable for service providers towards the end of the contract to swap staff, just when continuity may be important. With an eye to the future, the parties might wish to determine whether the Acquired Rights Directive and TUPE apply upon the expiry of the contract. Service providers might require the customer to enter into a contract with a new provider in a form under which the Directive of TUPE will apply.

There are also stringent labour laws in India that need to be considered. India offers statutory protection to employment, compensation, welfare and working conditions to a category of employees who may be categorised as "workman". The defining factor is the nature of the work undertaken by the employee. If it is supervisory or managerial in nature he / she may be considered excluded from the definition of "workman"[198]. Software engineers, call centre employees etc may fall within the definition (though there is little case law to substantiate).

Where employees are transferred from an EC country to an Indian service provider, it is possible that transferred employees are granted better protection under Indian labour laws than that offered in their home countries. This however should be something that a service provider's due diligence enquiry should clarify as an issue for the service provider and not necessarily the customer, although the customer's staff may get some comfort in knowing that their rights will be honoured by the receiving Indian service provider.

The next chapter discusses the compliance requirements for certain industries and how such obligations could be allocated within the contract.

198 Industrial Dispute Act 1947 (India) and Factories Act 1948 (India).

20. Legal and regulatory risks

This chapter discusses the compliance requirements for certain industries and how such obligations could be allocated within the contract.

20.1 Categorising legal and regulatory risks

Legal and regulatory issues commonly fall in two categories:

- Customers in regulated industries: banks or hospitals, for example – must comply with distinctive and often stringent regulatory requirements (for example, concerning privacy of customer and patient records). Changes in requirements may mean costly changes in outsourced systems and operations[199].
- Laws of general application affect customers and service providers alike. All employers, for example, must comply with employment laws and regulations. Some laws of general application assume greater importance in particular industries. Environmental laws, for example, may matter far more to an oil or chemical company than to a retailer.

Compliance is not optional. Most companies accept responsibility for their own compliance, and indemnify others for violations within their sphere of responsibility.

20.2 Planning for change

Complex questions arise when laws and regulations change, especially in regulated industries. Which party should track changes, and (at least implicitly) assume risks of non-compliance?

If a contract is silent, changes in law may be a force majeure event. If changes in law raise costs of performance, a service provider may claim compensation. Indeed, when changes dictate changes in systems, the service provider may see a sales opportunity.

---

[199] Outsourcing to India: Key Legal and Tax Considerations for US Financial Institutions: Baker and McKenzie, April 2004.

Service providers commonly propose that their regulated customers:

- Advise them of regulatory changes affecting the service.
- Give direction, in the form of business requirements, based on the customer's interpretation of regulatory requirements.

Costs of regulatory compliance often present negotiation challenges. Each side would naturally prefer to shift risks and costs of compliance to the other, but most recognise that regulatory changes are, like force majeure events, beyond either party's foresight or control.

Negotiated resolutions of these issues vary, depending upon the industry, the regulations' impact and other circumstances, but it is often useful to separate general costs of compliance – what the service provider must do to serve any and all customers affected by new regulations – from customer specific measures and plans.

20.3 Markets in Financial Instruments Directive (MiFID)

Europe's Markets in Financial Instruments Directive (MiFID) taking effect in November 2007, will bar securities firms from turning their compliance obligations over to third parties. This reform may affect how some activities are outsourced to India.

MiFID is one of the pillars of the European Union's Financial Services Action Plan, which is designed to create a single European market for financial services.

MiFID is intended to replace the current Investment Service Directive. Unlike that directive, MiFID is explicit in addressing the role and management of outsourcing within the financial services sector[200].

The key provision of MiFID for the outsourcing world is Article 13(5) of Level 1:

"An investment firm shall ensure, when relying on a third party for the performance of operational functions which are critical for the provision of continuous and satisfactory service to clients and the performance of investment activities on a continuous basis, that it takes reasonable steps to avoid undue additional operational risks. Outsourcing of operational functions may not be undertaken in such a way as to impair materially the quality of its internal control and the ability of the supervisor to monitor the firm's compliance with all obligations."

---

[200] MiFID follows the Lamfalussy legislative process: Level 1, which provides the overall framework of the directive, was first published in 2004, and in February of this year the Commission published its draft Level 2 measures for MiFID. Both levels were finalised in June 2006.

The Level 2 measures provide more detailed and practical guidance on how they envisage Article 13(5) should be implemented, including:

- No delegation of compliance: Where an investment firm delegates a function to a service provider, the responsibility for performance of such function remains with the management of the investment firm.
- Service Agreements: There must be a written agreement between the investment firm and the service provider, which provides for:
  - Delineation of the functions of the parties
  - Continuous monitoring (of, in particular, quality)
  - Mechanisms to manage and adjust services
  - Adequate termination of rights and remedies
  - Protection of client information
  - Appropriate business continuity and disaster recovery functions
  - Audit rights of the competent authority to audit service providers

There is an additional requirement if an institution outsourced any aspect of its asset management function for retail customers to a service provider in a country outside the European Economic Area. The investment firm must ensure that:

- The service provider is subject to prudential regulation.
- There is a mechanism for formal cooperation between the institution's regulator(s) and the regulator of the service provider.

For example, if a service provider in India provides back-office functions for the asset management part of a retail bank in London that is regulated by the FSA, then the service provider will need to enter into an agreement with the Reserve Bank of India to provide a mechanism for supervision.

The next chapter discusses some of the specific issues of importance in the context of outsourcing to India that should be considered as part of the outsourcing agreement.

21. Specific Indian legal issues of importance

This chapter discusses some of the specific issues of importance in the context of outsourcing to India that should be considered as part of the outsourcing agreement. Such factors include Taxation laws, Labour laws and others that will need to be considered as part of the agreement.

21.1 Taxation issues

The Indian Income Tax Act 1961 provides that a non-resident company in India will be taxed on:

- Income received or deemed to be received in India by it or on its behalf.
- Income that accrues or arises to it in India[201]

India grants special tax deductions and incentives for businesses which manufacture computer software[202] and are located in Special Zones, Electronic Hardware Technology Parks and Software Technology Parks.

The Indian Supreme Court has recently ruled on what constitutes goods and what constitutes as services within the IT sector. Both branded and unbranded software is considered "goods", while any service in relationship to software is considered "service"[203].

There is a distinction between core and non-core functions in Indian tax laws[204]. The outsourced company needs to ensure "Permanent Establishment" issues do not arise. The Indian Revenue department issued a clarification dated 2nd Jan 2004: *"If the outsourcing activities in India are non-core, i.e. incidental to the activities of the non-Indian outsourcer, no Indian tax would be levied on the foreign*

201 Income Tax Act 1961, S5(1)(a) and (b).

202 The Income Tax Act defines "computer software" as (i) any computer programme recorded on any disc, tape, perforated media or other information storage device; (ii) any customized electronic data or any product or service of similar nature as may be notified by the Board; and which is transmitted or exported from India to a place outside India by any means.

203 Income Tax Act 1961and Circular No 81/2/2005-ST.

204 Ibid.

outsourcer. However, if outsourcing activities in India are core activities of the foreign outsourcer, the global profits attributable to the activities of Indian outsourcing unit would be subject to tax in India".

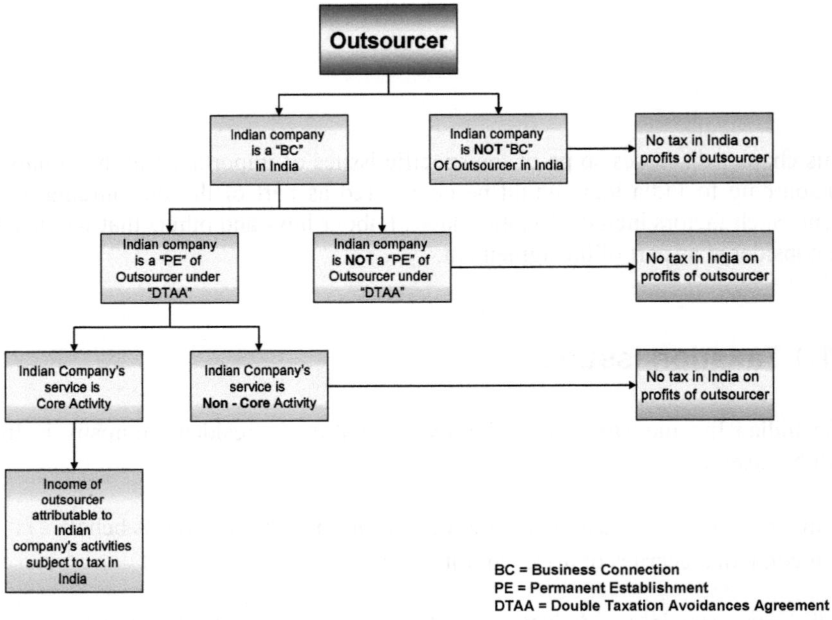

Fig .10. Taxation issues in India: adapted from Thaker and Thaker Advocates

Detailed transfer pricing regulations have also been introduced in India since 2001, by way of amendments to the Income Tax Act, 1961. These regulate international transactions between two or more associated enterprises, either or both of which are non residents and where transactions must be on an arm's length basis.

Payment of software including shrink wrap software may be considered royalty, therefore raising issues of taxability in India. Recently Income Tax appellate Tribunal at Bangalore in Lucent Hindustan's case[205] has accepted the distinction between "sale of copyright" and "sale of copyright product". Sale of shrink wrap software therefore is likely not to be considered royalty.

A customer should also examine whether it is required to withhold any local taxes upon remitting payments to the Indian service provider. In general where two countries have signed a tax treaty, the resident in one country is obligated to withhold any tax on remittances of "royalty, dividends or interest" to a resident of the other country.

205 Lucent Technologies Hindustan Ltd. v. ITO [2003] 92 ITD 366 (Bangalore).

If the customer intends to eventually acquire an operating unit of the local Indian service provider, it would ideally structure the acquisition as a share purchase in order to ensure retention of 100% tax holiday on export profits of the unit. An asset acquisition could result in a loss of tax incentives in India, because the Indian acquisition would likely not satisfy the conditions that

1. It uses at least 80% of the plant and equipment not previously used in India.
2. It is not a reconstituted of a business already in existence in India.

However a share purchase may have adverse employment law implications, because the customer is likely to inherit all the employees along with the accumulated benefits and seniority.

Another risk area is the move by governments to crack down on tax evasion and harmonize rules globally. The UK's insurance and outsourcing sector has been given brief reprieve from Value Added Tax (VAT) charges on outsourced services, but has been warned that charges will have to be imposed in the future. All European insurers are facing the prospect of having to pay VAT at 17.5% in the UK on all outsourced services, without being able to pass on the charge onto customers – something that no doubt would be followed by other European countries if this were to be imposed in the UK.

21.2 Employment laws

There is no single code or piece of legislation governing employment laws. Rather a number of statutes govern various labour and employment law issues. The most important statutes for the purposes of outsourcing are:

- The Industrial Dispute Act 1947 (broadly covers the investigation and settlement of disputes, retrenchments (termination), closures, lay-offs, strikes and lock-outs).
- The Industrial Employment (Standing Orders) Act 1946 (requires employers in industrial establishments formally to define conditions of employment or standing order to make employees aware of them).
- The various State enacted shops and establishments legislation (generally provides for conditions of employment in shops and other commercial establishments).

A European employee of a customer who temporarily relocates to India may be entitled to claim the protection of the Indian employment laws. Any such relocation raises a number of considerations under both the Indian and European laws. Indian visa requirements should be considered even for a short term transfer. The employee may be subject to Indian income tax although the UK and India tax treaty provides an exemption if:

1. The employee does not spend more than 182 days in India's tax year.
2. No costs are charged back to an Indian entity.

The employer and employee may also be required to make social security contributions in India.

21.2.1 Protection for workmen

Due to India's socialist past, Indian laws are pro-labour and Indian courts tend to be pro-labour in the case of "workmen". Employees are categorised according to the nature of the work performed and the fulfilment of certain prescribed criteria provided in the Industrial Disputes Act. The Act defines a "workmen" as *"any person (including an apprentice) employed in any industry to do any manual, unskilled, skilled, technical, operational, clerical or supervisory work for hire or reward, whether the terms of employment be express or implied"*

However, this definition excludes any person:

- Who is employed mainly in a managerial or administrative capacity.
- Those who being employed in supervisory capacities draws wages exceeding Rs1600 per month.
- Who exercises functions mainly of a managerial nature.
- Or those in the armed or police forces.

In the past, courts have interpreted this definition by holding that the designation of an employee is of little importance. Rather what is important is the nature of duties being performed by the employee, particularly his primary or basic duties and the dominant purpose of his employment.

In a recent case before the Supreme Court[206], the Court stated that *"In India, the test to determine whether a property is a good is not whether it is tangible or intangible, but whether the concerned item is capable of abstraction, consumption and use and whether it can be transmitted, transferred, delivered, stored, possessed etc. In the case of software, both canned and uncanned, all these are possible"*. In view of the inclusion of software in the definition of "goods", it is likely that software development will be considered a manufacturing process – accordingly large software companies will, in all likelihood fall under the applicability of the termination, closure and lay-off protection provisions of the Industrial Disputes Act.

---

[206] Statutory Protection for Software Development Workers, Trilegal, Anand Prasad and Biraj Tiwari.

India's labour laws will not apply to the foreign entity where there is no contractual relationship between that entity and the Indian employees. It must be clearly stated in the outsourcing agreement that any issue relating to the Indian employees is the sole responsibility of the Indian service provider. However, the more control a foreign entity has over the outsourcing enterprise - the more it may be subjecting itself to Indian labour laws.

21.2.2 Confidentiality provisions in employment contracts

Written employment contracts with confidentiality agreements are generally enforceable, but post termination non-compete restrictions are not. Typically, contracts take the form of letters, except in cases of very senior appointments or appointments of a sensitive or technical nature involving detailed terms and conditions. However, fixed term contracts are also permitted and many employers enter into such contracts, as it gives them the option of discontinuing or renewing terms of employment depending on business requirements. Aside from employment contracts and letters of appointment, employers may also issue employees with:

- Confidentiality or non-disclosure agreements.
- Non-compete agreements.
- Service bonds.
- Invention and proprietary rights assignment agreements.

These agreements are essentially executed to protect the employer's confidentiality and trade secrets, and in the case of service bonds or undertakings, to prevent any loss to the employer on account of the employee leaving the company after benefiting from the company's training period.

The enforceability of a non-compete agreement will depend on its degree of reasonableness. The agreement should not prohibit or restrict the employee unreasonably. The courts have held that the question of whether a covenant in an agreement is unreasonably wide, must be decided giving due consideration to:

- The nature of the agreement.
- The qualifications of the employee and the service he is expected to provide.
- Whether the employee could secure alternative work for a similar nature.

A non-compete covenant for the duration of an employment contract is not regarded as a restraint of trade, however the courts are likely to hold that post-termination non-compete covenants are a restraint of trade.

21.2.3 Women's employment rights

Certain Indian States impose restrictions on 24 hour working and employment of women during the evening shift.

Women who work in factories and offices are prohibited from working at night[207]. The Factories Act adopted in 1948 states that no woman shall be required or allowed to work in any factory except between the hours of 6 a.m. and 7 p.m., with the proviso that the hours may be varied provided that no woman may work between 10 p.m. and 5 a.m. However, the law itself provides ways in which this ban on night work of women can be circumvented.

The High Court however struck down the ban on night work for Women as unconstitutional in the Vasantha case[208], holding that the ban on night work was a restriction and not a case of affirmative action.

Meeting a longstanding demand for gender parity in the workforce, the Indian Cabinet approved, in March 2005, an amendment in the Factories Act 1948 to allow women employees to work late night shifts with employers providing adequate safeguards at workplace and while commuting. The Cabinet amendment, allows women to work between 10 pm and 6am, *"provided adequate safeguards in the factory as regards occupational safety and health, equal opportunity for women workers, adequate protection of their dignity, honour and safety and their transportation from the factory premises to the nearest point of their residence"* are made[209] [210].

Unlike many countries, India does not recognize the concept of "transfer of undertakings", which implies that the employees associated with a business or business unit automatically transfer to the buyer along with all accumulated benefits and seniority, even where the acquisition has been structured as an asset purchase.

The next chapter provides a summary of the main issues discussed in the book and serves as a useful checklist of the critical legal issues that an enterprise within the EU will need to consider when contemplating offshoring services to companies based in India.

---

207 Factories Act, 1948 and the Shops and Establishment Acts of different states. Women working in hospitals and in agriculture are exempt from such laws.

208 Vasantha R. v. Union of India, 2001 II LLJ 843 (Mad.).

209 Statement by Information & Broadcasting Minister, Jaipal Reddy.

210 Financial Services Authority (FSA): Offshore Operations Industry Feedback, April 2005.

22. Summary

This book has outlined the critical legal issues that an enterprise within the EU must consider when contemplating outsourcing services to companies based in India. As is the case with respect to any material agreement, the structure of an outsourcing agreement is a key issue because it embodies the rights, remedies, duties and obligations of the parties and provides a blueprint for the parties' relationship.

Typically, outsourcing contracts commonly consist of services agreements, supplemented by schedules that describe the services, service level commitments, charges, transitional arrangements and other particulars.

Typically within the agreements, there are two separate contracts, one for the transfer of existing business and one for the actual services outsourced. The "transfer of assets" agreement document deals with the transfer, where relevant, of any property, assets, employees and IP ("the Transfer Agreement"). The outsourcing services agreement document is used to record and reflect the service description, service levels and the customer and the vendor's roles and responsibilities during the term ("the Service Agreement").

Outsourcing arrangements are usually long term, and it is often difficult to fully anticipate, describe and manage contingencies and change conditions in the agreement. Therefore these agreements often include within the contract, broad procedures that describe the process the parties will follow when changes occur in the relationship, without having to re-write the contract. It is important for companies to appreciate from the outset that outsourcing agreements are more successful where companies view the relationship as long-term and based on mutual respect.

When contracts transcend national boundaries, the national legal regime of any single country becomes inadequate. When the parties to the contract are located in different countries, at least two systems of law impinge upon the transaction and the rules of International Law come into play. Under Indian Law, parties are free to stipulate their terms of contract and lay down the law by which the contract is to be governed. It is also possible to split a contract, to allow different parts to be governed by different laws – where there is an absence of choice, Indian courts determine "proper law" of contract.

The best way to ensure the application of a particular legal system to international contracts is to choose a particular law to govern this contract. However, European Companies outsourcing to India should be aware, that inclusion of forum selection clauses within the agreements, which allocate jurisdiction to European courts, may still end up litigating in India, if an Indian court decides that the interests of justice will be better served by trial in India.

Arbitration is an alternative to full scale courtroom litigation. However, the process of arbitration is not governed by a well established set of case law and rules like litigation, so waiting for a final award can often be lengthier and decisions can be unexpected, since the decisions are frequently based on compromise. Therefore if arbitration is provided in the contract, it should state that the arbitration is to be governed by the terms of the contract, and insert such other provisions as may be necessary to restrict the arbitrator from going off on a detour of his own.

India has a written contract Act and all agreements are subject to this statute and thus agreements must be carefully drafted in accordance with Indian law. One of the main issues that arise when agreeing contracts is the issue of enforcing non-compete provisions. India has stringent laws against restrictive trade practices and thus enforceability of stand alone non-compete provisions on termination of a contract are questionable.

Before signing the agreement, a preliminary transition plan should be initiated. Payments for transition related services should be contingent upon achievement of key milestones. Good outsourcing contracts include specific commitments to support transition to another service provider, or repatriation of operations to the customer, when the contract expires or terminates.

Critically, outsourcing contracts need to contain a comprehensive mechanism by which the parties can agree the scope and charging impact of any particular change. The change control mechanism is likely to contain procedures for proposing and accepting changes, as well as an escalation process for resolving disputes over the scope and pricing of any change.

The typical outsourcing engagement will last for a number of years and be governed by a contract setting the terms and conditions between the customer and service provider for the duration of their relationship. It is important to regularly measure whether that relationship is working, and how well. In this context, Service Level Agreements (SLAs) are established to describe the performance levels required of the service provider of each service or product provided (actually operational level metrics should describe the service expected, whereas service level agreements establish the thresholds beyond which penalties may apply – these tend to get somewhat confused within the industry).

All contracts inherently attempt to allocate risk and reduce liability, and outsourcing contracts are no different in this respect. However, parties must be cognisant that any attempt to reduce liability will be assessed with respect to the national laws prohibiting unfair terms e.g. the UK Unfair Contract Terms Act 1977.

It is foreseeable that a service provider will not perform all its obligations or meet all performance standards during the term of the outsourcing agreement. Imposing damages is a common remedy, but measuring damages for failures to perform obligations and meet performance standards can be difficult. Companies must ensure that damage and indemnity clauses are defined as narrowly as possible otherwise they may find enforcement of such clauses will become difficult.

Many companies suffer because they do not plan for what happens when the end date of the contract approaches. The outsourcing contract must state clearly what happens at the point of termination. The effects of termination should depend on the cause of termination. The rights and duties of each of the parties upon termination or expiration of the agreement should depend upon the circumstances of the termination. The agreement should set out the processes the parties will follow upon termination so that the transition is orderly.

When outsourcing to India, particular consideration should be given to the possibility that today's outsourcing service provider may become tomorrow's competitor. The customer may consider a set of non-predation clauses designed to protect it from such competition from the service provider - however India has very specific laws that prohibit clauses that have the effect of restraint of trade. Every agreement, by which anyone is restrained from exercising a lawful profession, trade or business of any kind, will to that extent be void in India.

Clauses addressing certain issues can not be governed by any other selected Law other than Indian Law. These include issues relating to IP transfer, registration and protection; real estate; labour law and bankruptcy – all of these are areas which have statutes governing them in India. Parties cannot by contract exclude the applicability of these statutes.

Increasingly, when considering any type of data processing by a service provider and where data is transferred to India for processing, the company must also consider how the laws (or lack of laws) may affect the processing and its rights with respect to the information. It must consider the EU law in respect of duties placed upon it as "data controllers".

Intellectual Property is usually an area where there is much debate. The outsourcing agreement should state clearly whether the customer or the service provider will retain ownership of any intellectual property that may be used or developed by the other party during the course of their relationship. The agreement should also address the issue of which party will own the results of any new developments or improvements. The agreement should also clearly state, where appropriate, that any work created by the employees of the service provider immediately pass to the customer.

Outsourcing agreements inevitably have staffing implications. The European Commission's Acquired Right Directive (and the Transfer of Undertakings (Protection of Employment) Regulations 1981 in UK and similar such regulations in other European countries) have the effect that the contract of employment can continue between the employee and the service provider. The regulations can apply regardless of the size of the transferred undertaking. Customers must be fully aware of the implications of such regulations, although, the impact may be more apparent upon service providers than customers.

There are also India specific factors that should be considered, which include taxation laws and rules, and particular note should be given to the stringent labour laws that are evident in India.

It is advised that a local Indian counsel be sought in respect of matters which may be governed by Indian Law. However, as the contract should be governed by European law, a European legal council should also be sought, to ensure the contract adheres to relevant local provisions for unfair contract terms, data protection, employee rights and relevant local case law.

Afterword - the future of outsourcing to India

As has been briefly touched upon, the outsourcing market to India has been growing exponentially over the past few years, pushed by organisations striving to survive in a increasingly competitive and challenging environment and pulled by the pro-outsourcing policies initiated by the Indian Government and the positive natural attributes of having a functioning democracy, thriving entrepreneurship, rule of law and a well educated, mobile and relatively cheap workforce.

The benefits from outsourcing are likely to continue to increase. These benefits include:

- Allows further focus of management's effort to the "core" function of the company.
- It allows the achievement of cost-savings.
- It enables the sharing of cost-savings achieved through economies of scale gained by the outsourcing service provider.
- It allows the achievement of higher levels of service and performance due to specialization of the service provider.
- It potentially allows a reduction of capital expenditure, particularly in the sphere of information technology services, management and general support systems.
- It allows sharing of new and improvements in older technology methods from the service provider to the customer.
- It potentially enables shorter times to market for a customer's services, due to a more flexible and responsive process for the outsourced services.

The question which many are asking, is whether India will continue to dominate and be a destination of choice, or will its own success ultimately lead to its demise, with employment and real estate costs becoming comparatively expensive relative to new-comers such as China. What however, is a major factor in India's favour , is its track record, its relatively strong legal institutions, and the genuine efforts being made to bolster laws as are relevant to outsourcing. Although its cost advantage over time will narrow, it will still be in absolute terms, much cheaper than Western countries.

Indian service providers are increasingly becoming global players and adopting many of the practices and cultural practices which are seen in the West. In addition, Indian service providers in the face of increasing competition and constant scrutiny from the sceptical West, is investing significantly on hiring and training the best calibre people within India, investing in ensuring maximum security for its clients data and increasingly moving up the value chain, so they are not only driving cost reduction for its customers, but also creating innovative systems and process which are enabling its clients to exploit revenue potential.

Negative resentment however will likely to continue as countries see local jobs transferred overseas. Clearly this is a PR exercise that India and rational policy makers in Western countries must embark upon.

For the benefits offered by outsourcing, companies outsourcing to India must however recognize that there are real risks involved, and allocating such risk through a well constructed contract is a crucial step in minimizing such risks.

Annex

1. Sample contract template - Checklist

Readers must note that the template is offered merely as an example. Every outsourcing agreement will be different and it is important that the agreement fully articulates the understanding of both parties.

It is therefore recommended that readers thoroughly investigate the risks that it wishes to and can in reality, allocate to the third party through the contract. There may be other risk factors which I have not included in this template, but which may be critical to a particular business or outsourcing agreement, and it is therefore important to seek independent advice on the outsourcing process, risk assessment and contractual undertakings before embarking upon the outsourcing process, for the risks of not doing so are extremely high.

The entire outsourcing agreement may be split into various sections, typically having a master agreement which incorporates the bulk of the contractual duties, with the detail contained in attachments or schedules to the Master agreement.

The contract should clearly at the outset, state which attachments form part of the agreement, list all items which are included as part of the agreement and which are delineated as being provided by or applicable to each party.

These may include applications software modules, operating systems software, data processing, telecommunications equipment, services, telecommunications facilities, performance standards, charges and fees, and other relevant detailed items.

If there is a work plan for the project, it should also be attached. The work plan should include both parties' responsibilities.

2. Sample contract template - Section 1: Framework contract for outsourcing

2.1 Background

For the purposes of this template, the Outsourcing party, the customer, is referred to as “OUTSOURCING CUSTOMER” and the outsourcer, the supplier is referred as “OUTSOURCING SERVICE PROVIDER”.

The agreement should start by clearly stating why the “OUTSOURCING CUSTOMER” wishes to outsource certain of its services and to receive from an OUTSOURCING SERVICE PROVIDER, for its own benefit, the outsourced services.

- Pursuant to a request for proposal dated “xxx” (the "RFP") the “OUTSOURCING CUSTOMER” specified the basis on which it would consider outsourcing certain services.
- By proposals dated “yyy” (including written clarifications and variations thereto) The “OUTSOURCING SERVICE PROVIDER” represented to the “OUTSOURCING CUSTOMER” that it has the experience and expertise to provide the services to meet “OUTSOURCING CUSTOMER” requirements described in the RFP.

2.2 Definitions

The agreement should start with a section which defines key terms used in the relationship to help avoid disagreement about those terms.

2.3 Contract management

The “OUTSOURCING SERVICE PROVIDER” has, amongst other things committed to:

1. Achieving the cost savings which are further described in this Agreement.
2. Delivering the services at the prices set out in the Charges Schedule based on the stated usage volumes.
3. Providing the outsourced service which requires the "OUTSOURCING SERVICE PROVIDER" to not only deliver the services so as to meet the service levels but to:
   - Report on the achievement and non-achievement of all service levels
   - Report on the achievement and non-achievement of all customer service levels to the "OUTSOURCING CUSTOMER"
   - Manage the resolution of all issues which arise between the "OUTSOURCING CUSTOMER" and the "OUTSOURCING SERVICE PROVIDER" to ensure that the customer service levels are delivered to the "OUTSOURCING CUSTOMER"
   - Take all steps reasonably necessary (including applying such additional resources as are reasonably necessary) to rectify any service failures and prevent the same or similar service failure from occurring;

- In reliance on the "OUTSOURCING SERVICE PROVIDER" commitments, its stated experience and expertise and the "OUTSOURCING SERVICE PROVIDER" proposal submitted, the "OUTSOURCING CUSTOMER" wishes to engage the "OUTSOURCING SERVICE PROVIDER" to provide the services on the terms set out below.
- Certain staff and contracts are to be transferred or made available by the "OUTSOURCING CUSTOMER" to "the OUTSOURCING SERVICE PROVIDER" in accordance with the "Transfer Agreement" to enable the "OUTSOURCING SERVICE PROVIDER" to provide the services.

And should there be a need for a guarantee:

- In consideration of the "OUTSOURCING CUSTOMER" agreeing to enter into this Agreement with the "OUTSOURCING SERVICE PROVIDER", the Guarantor has agreed to enter into the Guarantee to guarantee the full obligations of the "OUTSOURCING SERVICE PROVIDER" under this Agreement.

2.3.1 Contract commencement and duration

Outsourcing arrangements are usually long-term, e.g., 5-10 years, because the outsourcing service provider is replacing buyer internal staff, is making investments of its own that it intends to recoup over a long period of time, and is trying to lock the buyer in to a long term commitment.

- This Agreement shall not come into effect until the "Transfer Agreement" and the Guarantee have been executed.
- Subject to the above, this Agreement will commence on the effective date and, subject to earlier termination in accordance with this Agreement, shall continue

in force for a period of “X” years from the service commencement date expiring at “Y” anniversary of the service commencement date.

2.3.2 Contract renewal

There are often renewal clauses following the end of the term, locking the buyer into another long term, e.g., five years. The triggering of these clauses should be contingent upon the buyer’s written approval or the “outsourcing service provider” meeting certain performance standards during and at the end of the term.

- The “OUTSOURCING CUSTOMER” may, subject to the agreement of the “OUTSOURCING SERVICE PROVIDER” extend the Agreement for an additional period of “X” months beyond the expiry date by serving written notice on the “OUTSOURCING SERVICE PROVIDER” no later than “Y” months prior to the expiry date in which case the term of the Agreement shall automatically be deemed to be so extended on the terms and conditions which applied immediately prior to the expiry date.

2.3.3 Contract modification (change order process)

Since most business process outsourcing arrangements contemplate a relatively long-term relationship, it is important that the agreement address the procedures to be followed when circumstances change. The agreement must be sensitive to the interrelationship among price, the scope of service and service levels. To this end, the agreement should be cognisant of the following factors;

Since technology is changing constantly, outsourcing agreements need some flexibility to address new ideas, new buyer products, changes in technology, and other foreseeable problems.

The key element is the change order process. The standard process involves each party having the right to submit proposed changes in the system or services to the other party. The receiving party has to respond within a defined period and, if it accepts the change order request, a contract amendment is executed or the parties sign the change order to reflect agreement on the scope of and terms related to the change. If it is rejected, the work is not performed.

- The “OUTSOURCING CUSTOMER” should have the right to require the “OUTSOURCING SERVICE PROVIDER” to make certain changes, if required by statutory or regulatory changes or because the “OUTSOURCING SERVICE PROVIDER” is, practically speaking, the only one that can make the change, subject to reasonable and equitable schedule and pricing terms. The parties should agree on the changes in schedule and pricing; but, if they cannot agree within a defined time period, the “OUTSOURCING SERVICE PRO-

VIDER" should perform the work and the disagreement should go to dispute resolution.

2.3.4 Contract validity (merger, take-over, bankruptcy)

Either the outsourcing service provider or the outsourcing customer could experience a change in its structure during the term, e.g., being acquired, merged into another entity, consolidated, or some other change. The agreement should anticipate and include terms to address likely events.

- For example, the "OUTSOURCING CUSTOMER" should be allowed to continue using the outsourcer's software and services without additional charge or penalty if the "OUTSOURCING CUSTOMER" is acquired. Alternatively, the "OUTSOURCING CUSTOMER" may want to have the right to terminate the agreement in such a situation, without penalty.
- The "OUTSOURCING CUSTOMER" should prevent the "OUTSOURCING SERVICE PROVIDER" from assigning or transferring the outsourcing agreement without the "OUTSOURCING CUSTOMER's" prior written consent, although the "OUTSOURCING SERVICE PROVIDER" will want to be able to assign its rights if it is acquired by or merged into another entity. In this situation, the "OUTSOURCING CUSTOMER" may want to receive a discount due to likely cut-backs in staffing that occur in acquisitions or to prevent any cut-backs from being imposed by the new owner of the outsourcer.

2.3.5 Contract termination

There may be a number of triggers that could lead to contract termination, such as:

- Termination for Convenience by the "OUTSOURCING SERVICE PROVIDER" - Although rare, termination for convenience rights sometimes are included for an "OUTSOURCING SERVICE PROVIDER". In such a case, the "OUTSOURCING SERVICE PROVIDER" would notify the "OUTSOURCING CUSTOMER" a long time in advance (e.g., 180 days) and allow the "OUTSOURCING CUSTOMER" to recover its costs, such as for equipment that could not be used by a replacement "OUTSOURCING SERVICE PROVIDER".
- Termination for Material Default - Each party should have the right to terminate for the other party's material default. Sometimes default events are delineated in the agreements, e.g., non-payment or failure to meet performance standards. However, each allegedly defaulting party should have the right to cure its material default, e.g., on 30 days' notice describing the default, to avoid the termination. In some mission critical systems, the "OUTSOURCING CUSTOMER" may limit the "OUTSOURCING SERVICE PROVIDER's" abi-

lity to terminate the agreement only due to the "OUTSOURCING CUSTOMER's" failure to make a material payment (instead of any material breach) within a significant time period (e.g., 90 days) after its due date and receipt of notice of non-payment.

- Termination of Agreement by either Party for Insolvency - The Agreement may be terminated by either Party with immediate effect by written notice to the other Party if any of the following events occurs in respect of the other Party:
  - a proposal is made for a voluntary insolvency.
  - a shareholder's meeting is convened for the purpose of considering a resolution that it be wound up or a resolution for its winding-up is passed.
  - a petition is presented for its winding up or for the making of an administration order, or an application is made for the appointment of a provisional liquidator.
- Termination of Agreement for Change in Control and Change of Focus - The Agreement may be terminated with immediate effect by written notice if:
  - There is a change in the control of the "OUTSOURCING SERVICE PROVIDER" or the "Guarantor"
  - The "OUTSOURCING SERVICE PROVIDER" ceases to be a global outsourcing service provider whether by reason of change in business focus, disposal, reorganisation or otherwise ("change in focus")
- Partial Termination for Default – the "OUTSOURCING CUSTOMER" may be entitled to terminate one or more of the service bundles without compensation to the "OUTSOURCING SERVICE PROVIDER" by notice to the "OUTSOURCING SERVICE PROVIDER" where there has been a consistent failure in respect of any service forming a material part

2.3.6 Important factors to include within the contract

- Transition - It is common for an "OUTSOURCING CUSTOMER" to replace the "OUTSOURCING SERVICE PROVIDER" at the end of the term or to bring the work back in-house. Therefore, plan as part of the initial contract for transitioning out to a new "OUTSOURCING SERVICE PROVIDER" or for services or a new system to be provided by the "OUTSOURCING CUSTOMER". Technology transfer during the course of the relationship will minimize risks when the arrangement ends. The "OUTSOURCING CUSTOMER" should also be able to hire the "OUTSOURCING SERVICE PROVIDER's" staff.
- Right of the "OUTSOURCING CUSTOMER" to continue using software - If the "OUTSOURCING SERVICE PROVIDER" is licensing the "OUTSOURCING CUSTOMER" the "OUTSOURCING SERVICE PROVIDER"'s software during the outsourcing arrangement and the "OUTSOURCING CUSTOMER" wants to keep using it following the outsourcing services term, the agreement should address costs, if any, of allowing the "OUTSOURCING CUSTOMER" to keep using the software after termination.

- Obligation of the “OUTSOURCING SERVICE PROVIDER” to continue maintaining its software - Again, if the software is owned by the “OUTSOURCING SERVICE PROVIDER”, the agreement should require the “OUTSOURCING SERVICE PROVIDER” to continue to maintain the software following termination of the outsourcing services according to a standard maintenance agreement (with limits on fee increases and other clearly articulated “OUTSOURCING SERVICE PROVIDER” obligations and “OUTSOURCING CUSTOMER” protections).

2.3.7 Acceptance procedures

For most outsourcing arrangements, the “OUTSOURCING SERVICE PROVIDER” will be replacing existing staff, systems or another “OUTSOURCING SERVICE PROVIDER”. As part of the replacement process, the agreement usually includes a procedure for determining when the new systems can replace older ones. The parties often pursue a design, development and review process where both contribute in different ways to implementing the new arrangement. The work plan or a statement of work includes charts or text describing each party’s responsibilities in this process.

Then the parties conduct the tests which are based on certain predefined criteria which are applicable to the type of outsourcing arrangement.

2.4 Law and place of jurisdiction

- This Agreement will be governed by and construed in accordance with the laws of “Country X” and each Party hereby submits to the exclusive jurisdiction of the “Country X” courts.

2.5 Transition-in

Transition principally concerns the activities to be carried out by the outsourcing service provider prior to the service commencement date in order to enable the outsourcing service provider delivery of the services in accordance with the Agreement.

- The “OUTSOURCING SERVICE PROVIDER” will, amongst other activities, undertake initial planning for transition and finalise its operational plans and implement each of the transition projects.

- During the transition period the "OUTSOURCING SERVICE PROVIDER" shall develop an infrastructure that will support continuous improvement throughout the term.

2.5.1 The Transition plan

The Transition Plan details the activities to be carried out by the outsourcing service provider (the "Transition Activities") during the Transition Period to ensure an orderly and efficient migration and delivery of the services to the outsourcing service provider (including implementation of required organisations, processes and technology).

The following factors must be considered in the transition planning:

- Transition projects.
- Transition timing, pre condition to service commencement and project completion schedules.
- Dependencies.
- Transition governance, including management and approvals process.
- Change management.

2.6 Employees

Many of the outsourcing customer employees will no longer be needed by the outsourcing customer, depending on the scope of outsourcing.

Some of them will be hired by the outsourcing service provider or terminated, with resulting employment law issues.

A core group of outsourcing customer employees will still be needed to manage and oversee the activities of the outsourcing service provider. If the outsourcing customer retains some responsibilities, those staff should be responsive to the outsourcing customer's requests for assistance and coordinate applicable activities with the outsourcing customer.

2.6.1 Transferring employees

If the outsourcing service provider is going to hire the outsourcing customer employees as its own (as opposed to using the outsourcing customer employees as seconded employees or independent contractors), then the agreement should set forth the parties' understanding with respect to the following:

- How many offers of employment will the "OUTSOURCING SERVICE PROVIDER" make to the "OUTSOURCING CUSTOMER" employees (if any).
- Will there be any sign-on or retention bonuses to facilitate access to personnel and institutional knowledge.
- Will the "OUTSOURCING SERVICE PROVIDER" require the "OUTSOURCING CUSTOMER" employees to complete employment applications and to go through the "OUTSOURCING SERVICE PROVIDER" typical hiring process.
- What are the terms under which the "OUTSOURCING SERVICE PROVIDER" will hire the "OUTSOURCING CUSTOMER" employees.
- What percentage of employees must join the "OUTSOURCING SERVICE PROVIDER" and what happens if this percentage is not met.
- What effect will any employee termination, transfer or relocation laws (e.g EU Directive and TUPE) have.
- What level of compatibility is there between each of the parties' employment policies.
- What happens to employees upon expiration or termination of the agreement.
- What restrictions will there be on hiring the other party's employees.
- What background checks must be run on the "OUTSOURCING SERVICE PROVIDER" employees and, for offshore outsourcing, what type and quality of background checks are even available.

2.6.2 Transferred employees

The agreement should address several issues regarding the provision of benefits to the employees transferred from the outsourcing customer to the outsourcing service provider, including:

- Accrued vacation time and vacation policies.
- Retirement plans and policies.
- Severance availability and policies.

2.6.3 Seconded employees

Seconded employees are those employees of a party that such party "lends" to the other party for some period of time. The parties will need to determine who will bear the actual economic responsibility for the seconded employees' compensation and benefits, and who will have the authority with respect to the replacement or termination of seconded employees.

2.6.4 Independent contractor agreement

The agreement should specify which party will be responsible for obtaining consents for the transfer of any relevant independent contractor agreements.

2.6.5 Terminated employees

There will be a host of issues to be considered if employees are to be terminated. Clearly will be dependent on the national employment laws in each customer host country.

2.7 Conflict resolution

The agreement should have a defined dispute resolution process. Quickly escalating disputes up the chain of management often resolves problems prior to litigation and is a recommended approach. Pending resolution of the dispute, however, the outsourcing service provider should continue performing its services. If the parties cannot resolve this dispute within a pre-defined time period, e.g., 30 days, either one should be entitled to pursue its other available remedies.

- Neither Party should be entitled to commence or pursue legal proceedings under the jurisdiction of the courts in connection with any such dispute until "X" days after the Dispute Resolution Procedure will have been deemed to be exhausted in respect of such dispute.
- The immediately preceding paragraph should not prevent a party from applying for injunctive relief in the case of:
  (a) Breach or threatened breach of confidentiality.
  (b) Infringement or threatened infringement of its Intellectual Property Rights or
  (c) Infringement or threatened infringement of the Intellectual Property Rights of a third party, where such infringement could expose the Party in question to liability.

Any question or difference which may arise concerning the construction, meaning or effect of this Agreement, or any matter arising out of or in connection with this Agreement will in the first instance be referred for resolution under the Dispute Resolution Process.

2.7.1 Escalation procedure

The management levels at which a dispute may be discussed need to be defined within the contract and should include time limits for each step in the escalation ladder. The process should also fully describe when a dispute is formally initiated

2.8 Rights and obligations

2.8.1 General and specific obligations and warranties

- The agreement must include a general warranty of the level at which the "OUTSOURCING SERVICE PROVIDER" will perform the services in accordance with industry standards. The "OUTSOURCING SERVICE PROVIDER" will want a standard of workmanship performance. The "OUTSOURCING CUSTOMER" may also want to include a warranty that the "OUTSOURCING SERVICE PROVIDER" will give the "OUTSOURCING CUSTOMER's" work a high priority.
- If the "OUTSOURCING SERVICE PROVIDER" is licensing the "OUTSOURCING CUSTOMER" software, the "OUTSOURCING SERVICE PROVIDER" should warrant that the software will perform in accordance with "specifications." Specifications should be defined to include all the standards and measurements upon which the "OUTSOURCING CUSTOMER" based its purchase, including the "OUTSOURCING SERVICE PROVIDER's" technical and user documentation, published specifications, brochures and sales materials used to induce the sale, the RFP issued by the "OUTSOURCING CUSTOMER" for the arrangement, proposals submitted by the "OUTSOURCING SERVICE PROVIDER" in response to the RFP, and performance standards established for the "OUTSOURCING SERVICE PROVIDER".
- The "OUTSOURCING SERVICE PROVIDER" will want the warranty to include qualifiers, i.e., that the software will perform "substantially" or "materially" in accordance with specifications. These qualifiers can increase the likelihood of a dispute over what is substantial and then over what the "OUTSOURCING SERVICE PROVIDER" needs to fix.
- The "OUTSOURCING SERVICE PROVIDER" should also warrant that its software and the equipment will not infringe or misappropriate any third-party's intellectual property rights, including patents, copyrights, trademarks or trade secrets. The "OUTSOURCING CUSTOMER" should obtain an indemnity against a claimed or actual breach of these warranties.

2.8.2 Remedies for failures to perform obligations or meet standards

It is foreseeable that an outsourcing service provider will not perform all of its obligations or meet all performance standards during the term of an outsourcing agreement. Therefore, the outsourcing customer should include remedies to address the most likely breaches of the outsourcing service provider. Imposing damages is a common remedy, but measuring damages for failures to perform obligations and to meet performance standards can be difficult. Nonetheless, the outsourcing service provider should meet all the standards and should compensate the outsourcing customer if it fails to perform as promised.

"OUTSOURCING SERVICE PROVIDER" obligations

- One way to address this practical problem about quantifying the harm from the "OUTSOURCING SERVICE PROVIDER" failure to meet performance standards is to get a credit for each failure of the "OUTSOURCING SERVICE PROVIDER" to meet each performance measurement. The credit has to be compensatory.
- "OUTSOURCING SERVICE PROVIDER" providing more comprehensive outsourcing will propose outsourcing arrangements based on their estimates of, among other factors, the "OUTSOURCING CUSTOMER's" likely processing volumes over the term of the agreement. The "OUTSOURCING CUSTOMER" will often be providing its estimates of volume.
- Although universally disliked by "OUTSOURCING SERVICE PROVIDER"s, liquidated damages are possible to obtain in outsourcing arrangements. They should be carefully and narrowly crafted.

"OUTSOURCING CUSTOMER" obligations

- In all cases, the "OUTSOURCING CUSTOMER" will still be responsible to Regulators. As a result, the "OUTSOURCING SERVICE PROVIDER" will be reporting to the "OUTSOURCING CUSTOMER" staff which retains its responsibilities to report to upper management about information technology activities.
- The "OUTSOURCING CUSTOMER" will in all cases also be required to report problems and needs to the "OUTSOURCING SERVICE PROVIDER". If the "OUTSOURCING CUSTOMER" operations are being affected by a technical problem, the "OUTSOURCING CUSTOMER" will have to report such problems to the "OUTSOURCING SERVICE PROVIDER" within a certain period of time or risk waiving the right to require the "OUTSOURCING SERVICE PROVIDER" to repair the problem as part of its services and at no additional cost.

- An "OUTSOURCING CUSTOMER" will also need to warrant that the software it provides to the "OUTSOURCING SERVICE PROVIDER" doesn't infringe or violate any intellectual property rights of third parties and works as required for the "OUTSOURCING SERVICE PROVIDER" to do its job.

2.9 Confidentiality

Each Party should recognise that under the Agreement it may receive or become appraised of information belonging or relating to the other. All such information which is designated as confidential or is otherwise clearly confidential in nature constitutes "Confidential Information" for the purposes of the Agreement.

Each Party should agree

- Not to divulge Confidential Information belonging to the other to any third Party (including a sub-contractor) except to the extent, and for the purposes, expressly anticipated in this Agreement.
- Not to divulge Confidential Information belonging to the other to any of its employees who do not need to know it, without, in either case, the prior written consent of the other.
- Each Party should also agree to take all proper and reasonable measures (including taking all necessary security measures) to require that its employees and sub-contractors keep secret and treat as confidential all such Confidential Information. Where appropriate, and if so required by the other Party, such proper and reasonable measures shall include procuring that employees and sub-contractors shall each sign a non-disclosure agreement with the other Party in such reasonable terms as that Party shall prescribe.

The obligation in the preceding provisions should survive the termination or expiry of the Agreement for a period of "X" years.

2.10 Data and protection

- The "OUTSOURCING SERVICE PROVIDER" should not acquire any right in, or title to, any part of "OUTSOURCING CUSTOMER" Data. The "OUTSOURCING SERVICE PROVIDER" should not use or reproduce the "OUTSOURCING CUSTOMER" Data (whether or not such constitutes personal data) in whole or in part in any form except as may be required by the Agreement.
- The "OUTSOURCING SERVICE PROVIDER" shall process only the "OUTSOURCING CUSTOMER" Data and Personal Data on the "OUTSOURCING CUSTOMER" systems or any other systems used by the "OUTSOURCING SERVICE PROVIDER" to provide the services and undertakes not to process

any other data (other than the "OUTSOURCING CUSTOMER" Data and Personal Data) on the "OUTSOURCING CUSTOMER" systems or any other systems used by the "OUTSOURCING SERVICE PROVIDER" to provide the services without the prior written consent of the "OUTSOURCING CUSTOMER".

- The "OUTSOURCING SERVICE PROVIDER" may not delay, manipulate, divert, capture or interfere in any other way with any of the "OUTSOURCING CUSTOMER" data except when the "OUTSOURCING SERVICE PROVIDER" considers (and the "OUTSOURCING CUSTOMER" agrees) that it is necessary to do so in order to enable the "OUTSOURCING SERVICE PROVIDER" to continue to provide the services in accordance with the terms of the Agreement.
- The "OUTSOURCING SERVICE PROVIDER" should be responsible for maintaining, in accordance with the directions of the "OUTSOURCING CUSTOMER", secure copies of all the "OUTSOURCING CUSTOMER" data.
- Any "OUTSOURCING CUSTOMER" data which are lost or damaged due to "OUTSOURCING SERVICE PROVIDER" default shall be reinstated by the "OUTSOURCING SERVICE PROVIDER" or, at the "OUTSOURCING CUSTOMER" option, a third party appointed by the "OUTSOURCING CUSTOMER" to the last available back-up at the "OUTSOURCING SERVICE PROVIDER" cost and expense.
- The "OUTSOURCING SERVICE PROVIDER" shall reimburse the "OUTSOURCING CUSTOMER" in respect of any fines, charges or payments imposed by any Regulatory Authority, Data Protection Commissioner and/or any other similar body or entity as a result of any breach by the "OUTSOURCING SERVICE PROVIDER" of its obligations under this Agreement.
- The "OUTSOURCING CUSTOMER" hereby appoints the "OUTSOURCING SERVICE PROVIDER" as Data Processor and as agent of the "OUTSOURCING CUSTOMER" in relation to the Personal Data which the "OUTSOURCING SERVICE PROVIDER" Processes in order to perform the Services.
- The "OUTSOURCING SERVICE PROVIDER" will process the personal data in accordance with the relevant Data Protection Laws.
- The "OUTSOURCING SERVICE PROVIDER" warrants that it has appropriate operational and technological processes and procedures in place to safeguard against any unauthorised access, loss, destruction, theft, use or disclosure of the personal data.
- The "OUTSOURCING SERVICE PROVIDER" shall indemnify the "OUTSOURCING CUSTOMER" against all costs, expenses (including legal expenses), damages, loss, liabilities, demands, claims, actions or proceedings which the "OUTSOURCING CUSTOMER" may incur as a result of any breach by the "OUTSOURCING SERVICE PROVIDER" or its Subcontractors of its obligations under the Agreement as Data Processor.

2.11 Auditing and security requirements

2.11.1 Auditing

- The “OUTSOURCING SERVICE PROVIDER” should fully co-operate with and assist the “OUTSOURCING CUSTOMER” in meeting its audit, regulatory and security requirements. The “OUTSOURCING CUSTOMER” should provide written confirmation to the “OUTSOURCING SERVICE PROVIDER” of the identity of those third parties (if any) that it has authorised to conduct the audit.
- The “OUTSOURCING SERVICE PROVIDER” should provide access for the “OUTSOURCING CUSTOMER”, its internal auditors (which shall, for the purposes of this Agreement include the “OUTSOURCING CUSTOMER’s” internal audit, security and operational risk functions), its external auditors, any agents appointed by the “OUTSOURCING CUSTOMER” or its regulators (or any person appointed by such body) to conduct appropriate reviews and inspections of the activities and records of the “OUTSOURCING SERVICE PROVIDER” relating to the performance of the “OUTSOURCING SERVICE PROVIDER” obligations and to the charges (including access to any staff or information, including access to databases) for the purpose of reviewing and verifying, subject to confidentiality provisions.

2.11.2 Security

The “OUTSOURCING SERVICE PROVIDER” should:

- Make permanently available secure room(s) at the agreed premises. Such rooms should:
  - Have fully operational telecommunications line and network ports.
  - Have secure storage facility.
  - Have desks and other reasonable office facilities required by the “OUTSOURCING CUSTOMER”.
  - Not be accessed by anyone other than the “OUTSOURCING CUSTOMER” or persons approved by the “OUTSOURCING CUSTOMER”

2.11.3 Regulatory

- The “OUTSOURCING SERVICE PROVIDER” undertakes at all times to deal with Regulatory Authorities in an open and co-operative manner and at all times to act in accordance with any requirements, rules or guidance issued by the Regulatory Authorities or any such other body that are relevant to the provision of the services.

- For the avoidance of doubt, any examination or inspection by the "OUTSOURCING CUSTOMER" or its auditors or regulators shall not constitute a waiver or exclusion of any of the "OUTSOURCING SERVICE PROVIDER" obligations or the "OUTSOURCING CUSTOMER" rights under the Agreement.

2.11.4 Cost of review

- The "OUTSOURCING SERVICE PROVIDER" costs of a routine or emergency audit review shall be borne by the "OUTSOURCING SERVICE PROVIDER". The "OUTSOURCING SERVICE PROVIDER" shall additionally bear the audit costs of the "OUTSOURCING CUSTOMER" where any review (routine or emergency) finds material irregularities, material errors or material non-compliance on the part of the "OUTSOURCING SERVICE PROVIDER" or its Sub-contractors either with any statutory or regulatory requirements or with the terms of this Agreement but otherwise the "OUTSOURCING CUSTOMER" costs of review shall be borne by the "OUTSOURCING CUSTOMER".

2.11.5 Consequences of review

- The findings of any review shall be discussed and agreed by the relevant the "OUTSOURCING CUSTOMER" internal audit function and the "OUTSOURCING SERVICE PROVIDER" management under review and, in the absence of agreement, shall be referred to the Dispute Resolution Procedure.

2.11.6 Contingency planning for disaster

Organisations are very dependent on their IT infrastructure to support their business processes and deliver competitive advantage. If a disaster affects their ability to operate the IT infrastructure, business processes stop, and they lose market share. It is thus important to plan for potential disasters and how services are continued to be made available.

- Each Disaster Recovery Plan should incorporate at a minimum the existing processes and procedures and the infrastructure and personnel currently in place that the "OUTSOURCING SERVICE PROVIDER" will use in providing Disaster Recovery services, including information regarding disaster recovery planning and testing capabilities, disaster recovery invocation procedures, recovery site management and standard backup and recovery procedures. These plans should be updated and maintained by the "OUTSOURCING SERVICE PROVIDER" and be modified to reflect changes in Disaster Recovery requirements.

- Before any improved services recovery requirements are implemented, the "OUTSOURCING SERVICE PROVIDER" shall prepare and submit to the "OUTSOURCING CUSTOMER" for approval revised versions of the Disaster Recovery Plans to reflect and be consistent with the changes to the Disaster Recovery Services resulting from the implementation of the improved services recovery requirements
- The Disaster Recovery Plans shall be maintained and updated by the "OUTSOURCING SERVICE PROVIDER" so that they continue to reflect the contemporaneous state of the services being provided to the "OUTSOURCING CUSTOMER". The "OUTSOURCING SERVICE PROVIDER" shall incorporate into the Disaster Recovery Plans any amendments required as a result of changes agreed pursuant to the contract change process.

2.11.7 Disaster recovery testing

- The "OUTSOURCING SERVICE PROVIDER" shall carry out regular testing of the Disaster Recovery Services at the frequencies set out as appropriate and in accordance the Disaster Recovery Plans. The "OUTSOURCING SERVICE PROVIDER" may request a change to the regularity of tests following each annual review, providing reasons for the request, and the "OUTSOURCING CUSTOMER" will give the request reasonable consideration and may, in its absolute discretion, agree to any such request. Any resulting changes shall be dealt with using the contract change process.

Provision of disaster recovery services

- On the declaration of a Disaster by either of the Parties, the "OUTSOURCING SERVICE PROVIDER" shall:
  - take all such steps as are stipulated by the Disaster Recovery Plan in order to restore the supply of all Services directly affected by the Disaster.
  - achieve the recovery of the services in accordance with and within the recovery time-scale requirements set out in:
    1. in the case of a Disaster occurring prior to the implementation of improved services recovery requirements, the existing services recovery service levels; and
    2. in the case of a Disaster occurring on or after the implementation of improved services recovery requirements, the improved services recovery requirements
- Take such further steps as may reasonably be expected from the "OUTSOURCING SERVICE PROVIDER" as a leading supplier of such services and/or such steps as are at its disposal.
- Ensure that during the Recovery Period (as identified in the Disaster Recovery Plan) the services are provided in accordance with the Disaster Recovery Plan.

- Use all reasonable endeavours to ensure that all services indirectly affected by the Disaster continue to be provided in accordance with the service levels during the Recovery period.
- Ensure that all services which are not directly or indirectly affected by the disaster continue to be provided in accordance with the service levels.

2.11.8 Proprietary rights

- Products developed prior to the term - The "OUTSOURCING SERVICE PROVIDER" and the "OUTSOURCING CUSTOMER" will each own the works they bring to the arrangement. These will usually include software and printed materials, such as the "OUTSOURCING CUSTOMER" procedures or the "OUTSOURCING SERVICE PROVIDER" manuals and documentation. These arrangements usually continue during the term.
- Products developed during the term - The more difficult problem arises over products developed during the term. The "OUTSOURCING SERVICE PROVIDER" will want to own the actual products, as well as the intellectual property, e.g., ideas, concepts, inventions, etc., contained in the products. Depending upon the scope of the arrangement, these products may have been developed jointly by the technical staffs of both parties working together. Or, the "OUTSOURCING SERVICE PROVIDER" may develop a product, such as a software module, which contains the "OUTSOURCING CUSTOMER's" trade secrets (e.g., one of its procedures) or which could be packaged and licensed to other parties. In all of these cases, the parties should negotiate up-front the value, such as joint ownership, credits, reduced licensing fees, or royalties from the "OUTSOURCING SERVICE PROVIDER's" licensing to third parties of such software modules. Or, the "OUTSOURCING SERVICE PROVIDER" may just obtain a right of first refusal to purchase such modules.

2.12 Pricing / payment procedure

Pricing for outsourcing services will depend upon the nature and scope of the services. They could include the following:

- Flat amount - For outsourcing of services with predictable cost, time and processing volume requirements each month or other time period, the "OUTSOURCING SERVICE PROVIDER" will want a monthly fee which covers its costs and includes a profit margin.
- Per transaction fee - For outsourcing arrangements which are based on processing data for the "OUTSOURCING CUSTOMER", the "OUTSOURCING SERVICE PROVIDER" may want to be paid on a per transaction basis. The arrangement may include a fee escalator which allows the "OUTSOURCING

SERVICE PROVIDER" to increase its fees due to increased processing volume, or other conditions. The "OUTSOURCING SERVICE PROVIDER" may also set a "floor" so that its fees are a minimum amount, even if the volume drops below the floor.

- Compensation based on the "OUTSOURCING CUSTOMER's" results or other measurement - "OUTSOURCING SERVICE PROVIDERs"s may tie their fees (in part) into the "OUTSOURCING CUSTOMER" business results, subject to the "OUTSOURCING SERVICE PROVIDER" meeting certain conditions. If structured properly, this type of arrangement can provide significant incentives to the "OUTSOURCING SERVICE PROVIDER" to cut costs, while allowing the "OUTSOURCING SERVICE PROVIDER" and "OUTSOURCING CUSTOMER" to share the risks and benefits of this type of relationship
- Hourly rates - A rate schedule will often be added as an appendix for work that the "OUTSOURCING SERVICE PROVIDER" provides beyond the planned tasks. This schedule of hourly or other types of rates will also be used when the "OUTSOURCING SERVICE PROVIDER" makes proposals for providing additional services.
- Unless expressly stated otherwise in the Agreement, all charges set out in the schedule should be fixed for the Term and will not be subject to indexation, wage inflation or general inflationary increases during the Term. The "OUTSOURCING CUSTOMER" will not be obliged to pay any other charges save and except charges agreed pursuant to the service change request process and/or the contract change process.

2.12.1 Charging principles

The charges payable by the "OUTSOURCING CUSTOMER" may be calculated and determined in accordance with different charging models which apply to different service elements.

Asset depreciation

The depreciation of existing assets during the Term will be calculated by, and be the responsibility, of the "OUTSOURCING CUSTOMER". The "OUTSOURCING CUSTOMER" depreciation will not be incorporated within the unit prices.

Verification process

The charges may be reviewed and subject to adjustment in accordance with the provisions of the verification schedule.

Billing approaches

Service credits and Liquidated Damages may be applied in accordance with the Service Points and Liquidated Damages Schedule.

Disputed charges

The "OUTSOURCING CUSTOMER" may withhold payment of any charges that it disputes in good faith by notifying the "OUTSOURCING SERVICE PROVIDER" within "x" business days of receipt of the relevant invoice. Such notice shall set out the "OUTSOURCING CUSTOMER" reasons for disputing the invoice and specifying any additional information which it requires to resolve the disputed invoice.

The "OUTSOURCING SERVICE PROVIDER" shall continue to perform its obligations under this Agreement notwithstanding any withholding of payments. If the issue is not resolved with "x" Business Days the disputed element of an invoice shall be resolved in accordance with the Dispute Resolution Procedure.

2.13 Indemnities

The "OUTSOURCING SERVICE PROVIDER" will be controlling some vital aspect of the "OUTSOURCING CUSTOMER's" operations and infrastructure. In certain aspects of the relationship, the "OUTSOURCING SERVICE PROVIDER" should be willing to indemnify, defend and hold harmless the "OUTSOURCING CUSTOMER". They may include the following:

- Intellectual property.
  - The "OUTSOURCING SERVICE PROVIDER" should give these protections to the "OUTSOURCING CUSTOMER" in case the service provider has infringed copyrights, patents, or trademarks or misappropriated trade secrets.
  - The "OUTSOURCING CUSTOMER" will not know whether the service provider has wrongfully taken intellectual property from a third party until the "OUTSOURCING CUSTOMER" receives a claim, so the "OUTSOURCING SERVICE PROVIDER" should protect the "OUTSOURCING CUSTOMER" from all third party claims and actions, and should pay for all expenses and liability, resulting from any claim of infringement or misappropriation.
  - The "OUTSOURCING SERVICE PROVIDER" may prefer to just pay for amounts finally awarded by judgment.

- Injuries to persons or property caused by the "OUTSOURCING SERVICE PROVIDER".
  - It is common for the "OUTSOURCING SERVICE PROVIDER" to only give indemnities for injuries due to their negligence or wilful misconduct, or due to the equipment or their acts or omissions, unless the harm is caused by the "OUTSOURCING CUSTOMER's" negligence or wilful misconduct.
  - The "OUTSOURCING CUSTOMER" often give comparable indemnities to the "OUTSOURCING SERVICE PROVIDER", particularly if the "OUTSOURCING SERVICE PROVIDER" is operating systems located at the "OUTSOURCING CUSTOMER" site(s).
- Negligence and willful misconduct. The "OUTSOURCING CUSTOMER" may be able to receive a general indemnity from a "OUTSOURCING SERVICE PROVIDER"'s negligence or willful misconduct.
- Compliance with Laws and Regulations. The "OUTSOURCING SERVICE PROVIDER" often represents and warrants that they will comply with applicable laws and regulations in the performance of their duties. The "OUTSOURCING SERVICE PROVIDER" may require the "OUTSOURCING CUSTOMER" to instruct the "OUTSOURCING SERVICE PROVIDER" about specific applicable regulations, such as in the banking or health care fields. A "OUTSOURCING SERVICE PROVIDER" would then indemnify the "OUTSOURCING CUSTOMER" for its breach of these warranties because of the risks to the "OUTSOURCING CUSTOMER" and the role the "OUTSOURCING SERVICE PROVIDER" plays at the "OUTSOURCING CUSTOMER".

2.14 Damage limitations

The "OUTSOURCING SERVICE PROVIDER" will want two types of damage limitations:

- A disclaimer of consequential, special, incidental and indirect damages, including without limitation lost profits and lost business opportunities.
- A total cap on its possible damages. This amount may be based on a monthly service charge.

These damage limitations for the "OUTSOURCING SERVICE PROVIDER" should be lifted for damages resulting from indemnity obligations, such as for harm to persons or property, intellectual property infringement or misappropriation, and breach of confidentiality obligations.

The "OUTSOURCING CUSTOMER" should also limit its damages to the same extent as the "OUTSOURCING SERVICE PROVIDER" and disclaim damages other than direct damages.

2.15 Third party access

If the "OUTSOURCING SERVICE PROVIDER" is using software licensed by the "OUTSOURCING CUSTOMER", there may be limitations in the license agreements prohibiting third-party access, i.e., the "OUTSOURCING SERVICE PROVIDER" as a contractor may not be allowed access to another company's software. Or, the "OUTSOURCING CUSTOMER" may have to pay an additional fee. The "OUTSOURCING CUSTOMER" will need to get consent from those software providers to allow access by the "OUTSOURCING SERVICE PROVIDER", possibly at some additional cost.

2.16 Subcontracting

It is likely that the "OUTSOURCING SERVICE PROVIDER" will not be able to perform all its tasks by itself. Subcontracting of tasks, such as equipment and operating system software maintenance, is common because the service providers of those products are often more familiar with the products and more efficient in maintaining them. The agreement with the "OUTSOURCING SERVICE PROVIDER" should require that the "OUTSOURCING SERVICE PROVIDER" to be responsible and liable for the acts and omissions of any and all subcontractors. If the level of responsibility or risks created by the subcontractor is high the "OUTSOURCING CUSTOMER" will want to include an indemnity from the "OUTSOURCING SERVICE PROVIDER" for the acts and omissions of the subcontractor. The "OUTSOURCING CUSTOMER" may also want to receive copies of the subcontracts and to be included as a third party beneficiary which can enforce the terms of the subcontract if the prime contractor.

2.16.1 Rights to assign

Neither Party should be entitled to assign its rights or obligations under the Agreement without the prior written consent of the other Party

2.16.2 Approval of sub-contractors

- The "OUTSOURCING SERVICE PROVIDER" should not subcontract or delegate any of its obligations under the Agreement to a third party unless such third party has been reviewed by "OUTSOURCING CUSTOMER" and written approval is given by the "OUTSOURCING CUSTOMER" to the proposed subcontracting
- Sub-contracting of its obligations should not relieve the "OUTSOURCING SERVICE PROVIDER" of any liability for its performance under the Agreement. The "OUTSOURCING SERVICE PROVIDER" should remain liable at

all times for all acts or omissions of the Sub-contractor, and in particular, any act or omission which would be a default under this Agreement had it been done by the "OUTSOURCING SERVICE PROVIDER" should be deemed to be a default by the "OUTSOURCING SERVICE PROVIDER" under the Agreement notwithstanding the fact that it was done by the Sub-contractor and not the "OUTSOURCING SERVICE PROVIDER".

- Prior to entering into any subcontract with a Sub-contractor, the "OUTSOURCING SERVICE PROVIDER" should give the "OUTSOURCING CUSTOMER" written notice specifying the identity and qualification and experience of the third party and the nature and proposed scope of the subcontracting.
- The "OUTSOURCING SERVICE PROVIDER" should ensure that its subcontract with any Sub-contractor should include provisions equivalent to the provisions in the Agreement to the extent applicable to the "OUTSOURCING SERVICE PROVIDER" should ensure that all Sub-contractors adhere to the standards, policies and procedures in effect at the time, whether these are the "OUTSOURCING CUSTOMER" or the "OUTSOURCING SERVICE PROVIDER".

2.17 Insurance

The "OUTSOURCING SERVICE PROVIDER" should be required to obtain adequate insurance to provide financial protection for the indemnifications it provides to the "OUTSOURCING CUSTOMER". This would include: errors and omissions insurance or professional liability insurance to protect against the "OUTSOURCING SERVICE PROVIDER's" negligence; liability insurance for injuries and death; and worker's compensation insurance.

- At its own cost and expense the "OUTSOURCING SERVICE PROVIDER" should during the period of the Agreement and for a period of one year following its termination maintain in full force or procure such that there is maintained in full force for the benefit of the "OUTSOURCING SERVICE PROVIDER" and the "OUTSOURCING CUSTOMER" the following insurance cover:
  - Public Liability Insurance cover and Employer Liability Insurance cover up to a combined limit (for any single event or series of related events in a twelve month term) of £ XX.
  - Fidelity Guarantee (or Employee Dishonesty which shall for the avoidance of doubt include Employee Fraud) Insurance cover up to a limit (for any single event or series of related events in a twelve month term) of £ XX.
  - And shall ensure that the appropriate noting of the "OUTSOURCING CUSTOMER" interest has been recorded on the policies or a generic interest clause has been included if such action is required.

- During the period of the insurance cover referred, the “OUTSOURCING SERVICE PROVIDER” shall:
  - Do nothing knowingly to invalidate any such insurance policy or policies and preserve the “OUTSOURCING SERVICE PROVIDER” interest in such policy or policies.
  - On the written request of the “OUTSOURCING CUSTOMER” from time to time send certificates of insurance and confirmation of continued cover to the “OUTSOURCING CUSTOMER”.
  - Administer the insurance policy or policies and the “OUTSOURCING SERVICE PROVIDER” relationship with its insurers at all times to preserve the benefits for the “OUTSOURCING CUSTOMER” set out in this Agreement and shall use all reasonable efforts to procure that the terms of such policy or policies shall not be altered in such a way as to diminish the benefit to the “OUTSOURCING CUSTOMER” of such policy or policies.

2.18 Taxes

If there is a transfer of assets from the “OUTSOURCING CUSTOMER” to the “OUTSOURCING SERVICE PROVIDER”, such as the sale of equipment or software licenses, there may be taxes that need to be paid as part of the transaction and the responsibility for such payment needs to be set out in the contract.

2.19 Force Majeure

The Agreement should include a provision that neither party has liability for delays or failures to perform that are caused by events outside the reasonable control of the party, including the acts or omissions of the other party.

- Subject to the remaining provisions of this clause, to the extent that either Party is prevented from performing its obligations under this Agreement by an event beyond the Party in question's reasonable power to control (an "Event of Force Majeure") then that Party's obligation to perform its obligations under this Agreement will (during the continuation of the Event of Force Majeure) be read and construed as an obligation to perform such obligations to the best level reasonably achievable in the circumstances of the Event of Force Majeure provided that where the “OUTSOURCING SERVICE PROVIDER” claims that it is affected by an Event of Force Majeure, then such claim will only be valid to the extent that a prudent supplier could not have foreseen and prevented or avoided the effect of such event or occurrence.

2.19.1 Factors to constitute Force Majeure

- Notwithstanding the above clause, the following shall not be deemed to constitute an Event of Force Majeure for the purposes of this Agreement:
  - Deliberate sabotage of, or malicious damage to, equipment or data attributable to the "OUTSOURCING SERVICE PROVIDER", its employees or sub-contractors.
  - Labour disputes (including industrial strikes).
  - Any event which a prudent services provider, operating to good industry standards, could reasonably have foreseen and prevented or avoided.

2.19.2 Effect of suspension of service

To the extent that any Event of Force Majeure affecting the "OUTSOURCING SERVICE PROVIDER" results in any service being suspended, then the "OUTSOURCING CUSTOMER" may, at its sole discretion, require that any of the following options applies (and may change the option from time to time):

- The "OUTSOURCING CUSTOMER" will have no liability to pay charges in respect of such service for the period of such suspension.
- The "OUTSOURCING CUSTOMER" may direct the "OUTSOURCING SERVICE PROVIDER" to procure the provision of such service from an alternative supplier until cessation of the suspension.
- The "OUTSOURCING CUSTOMER" may direct the "OUTSOURCING SERVICE PROVIDER" to provide such alternative services (during the period of the suspension) as will be reasonably required to minimise the commercial disruption and losses suffered by the "OUTSOURCING CUSTOMER" as a result of the suspension.

provided that:

- if the period of suspension lasts for more than "X" days, the "OUTSOURCING CUSTOMER" will have the option, at the end of such period, to give notice terminating the service affected by the suspension forthwith

3. Sample contract template - Section 2: Description of services to be outsourced

3.1 Definitions

Start with a section which defines key terms used in the relationship to help avoid disagreement about those terms.

3.2 Description of the service

The scope of the services to be outsourced is a key issue because of the greater potential for conflict or ambiguity stemming from imprecise or ambiguous terms.

The specification of the scope of services should be as clear as possible at the time of execution of the Agreement because the scope of the services affects many other critical aspects of the agreement, such as pricing, service levels, warranties and exclusivity.

The specification of the scope of services should include the following:

- All functions that the parties intend to expressly include within the scope of services.
- All functions that the parties intend to expressly exclude from the scope of services.
- All functions that are the responsibility of the "OUTSOURCING CUSTOMER" or third parties.
- All dependent services (i.e., those functions that the "OUTSOURCING SERVICE PROVIDER" must perform that are contingent upon the performance of the "OUTSOURCING CUSTOMER" or a third party's responsibilities).
- All assumptions regarding the scope of services.

3.3 Service level agreement

- A service level agreement describes the performance levels required of the "OUTSOURCING SERVICE PROVIDER" for each service or product provided by the "OUTSOURCING SERVICE PROVIDER". Performance standards can be extensive if a "OUTSOURCING CUSTOMER" wants to manage processes, or they can be limited to a few key standards if the relationship is purely results-based.
- The "OUTSOURCING CUSTOMER" also needs to do projections of the growth of its service utilisation over the term of the Agreement. The "OUTSOURCING SERVICE PROVIDER" should warrant that the performance standards will be met for the "OUTSOURCING CUSTOMER" as its service utilisation grows, not just for the amount of utilisation at the time of contracting.

4. Sample contract template – schedules

The following list of schedules may need to be part of the Agreement:

1. Corportate Schedule
2. Operational Model Schedule
3. Service Provider Proposal to RFP Schedule
4. Licences Schedule
5. Governance Schedule
6. Asset Management Schedule
7. Inherent Defects Schedule
8. Transfer of Assets Schedule
9. Transfer of Employment Schedule
10. Transition-In Planning Schedule
11. Transition-Out Planning Schedule
12. Responsibility Matrix Schedule
13. Bencharking Procedure Schedule
14. Guarantee Schedule
15. Insurance Schedule
16. Data and Data Protection Schedule
17. Confidentiality Schedule
18. Quality Management Process Schedule
19. Arbitration Schedule
20. Information Technology and Systems Schedule
21. Intelletual Property Rights Schedule
22. Change Mangement (Order) Process Schedule
23. Pricing and Charging Schedule
24. Payment Schedule
25. Verification Schedule
26. Dispute Resolution Schedule
27. Escalation Schedule
28. Service Points and Liquidated Damages Schedule
29. Disaster Recovey Plan
30. Exit Management Schedule
31. Novation Schedule
32. Third Party Contracts Schedule
33. Sub-Contracting Schedule

34. Security Schedule
35. Testing Schedule
36. Auditing Schedule
37. Regulatory and Legal Obligations Schedule

References and resources

Statutes and international conventions

1. Acquired Rights Directive (Directive 77/187), now replaced by Directive 2001/23 (EC)
2. Arbitration and Conciliation Act of 1996 (India)
3. Article 29 Working Party (DGXV D/5025/98 WP 12)
4. Article 29 Working Party's Working document on a common interpretation of Article 26(1) of Directive 95/46/EC (2093/05/EN – WP114) (EC)
5. Civil Evidence Act 1972 (India)
6. Code of Civil Procedures 1908 (India)
7. Commission Decision 2002/16/EC dated 27 December 2001 (EC)
8. Community Patent Convention 1975
9. Competition Act 1998 (UK)
10. Data Protection Act 1998 (UK)
11. Directive 93/13 EEC, OJ 95, 21/4/93 (EC)
12. European Data Protection Directive (EC)
13. European Patent Convention 1978
14. Factories Act 1948 (India)
15. Industrial Employment (Standing Orders) Act 1946 (India)
16. Industrial Dispute Act 1947 (India)
17. Income Tax Act 1961 (India)
18. Markets in Financial Instruments Directive (MiFID) taking effect in November 2007
19. Misrepresentation Act 1967 (UK)
20. New York Convention, 1958
21. Sale and Supply of Goods Act 1994 (UK)
22. Sales of Goods Act 1979 (UK)
23. Supply of Goods and Services Act 1982 (UK)
24. The Contracts (Rights of Third Party) Act 1999 (UK)
25. The Consumer Protection Act of 1986 (India)
26. The Copyright Act, 1957 (India)
27. The Copyright (Amendment) Act, 1999 (India)
28. The Berne Convention 1886
29. The Indian Contract Act of 1872 (India)
30. The Indian Penal Code of 1960 (India)
31. The Information Technology Act of 2000 (India)
32. The Locarno Agreement 1968
33. The Madrid Agreement 1891
34. The Nice Agreement 1957
35. The Paris Convention for the Protection of Industrial Property 1883
36. The Restrictive Trade Practices Act 1976 (??)

37. The Sale and Supply of Goods to Consumers Regulations 2002 (EC)
38. The Specific Relief Act of 1963 (India)
39. The Strasbourg Agreement 1971
40. The Universal Copyright Convention 1952
41. Transfers of Undertakings Directive (2001/23) (EC)
42. Transfer of Undertakings (Protection of Employment) Regulations 1981 (TUPE) (UK)
43. Treaty of Rome (Articles 81 and 82) (EC)
44. Unfair Contract Terms Act 1977 (UK)
45. Unfair Contract Terms Directive (93/13/EEC) (EU)
46. Unfair Terms in Consumer Contracts Regulations 1999 (EC)
47. World Trade Organisation – (trade related aspects of intellectual property rights agreement 1994)

Case law

1. Air Foyle Ltd v Crosby-Clarke [2002] IRLR 483
2. Alisa Craig Fishing Ltd v Malvern Fishing Company [1983] 1 All ER 101 (HL)
3. All Bengal Transport Agency v Hare Krishna Bank, AIR 1985 Gau 7
4. Andrews v Hopkinson [1957] 1 QB 229
5. Asahi Metal Indus. Co v Superior Court, 480 U.S. 102, 115 (1987)
6. Astley v Celtec Ltd [2002] IRLR 629
7. Avery v Bowden [1855] 5 El & Bl 714
8. Ayse Suzen v Zehnacker Gebaudereinigung GmbH Krankenhausservice (C13/95) [1997] All E.R. (EC) 289 (ECJ)
9. Baldry v Marshall [1925] 1 KB 260
10. Banco de Portugal v Waterlow [1932] AC 452
11. Bangladesh Export Co v Sucden Kerry SA [1995] 2 Lloyds Rep 1.
12. Bannerman v White (1861) CB(NS) 844
13. Beckman v Dynamco Whiche Macfarlane Ltd. [2002] IRLR 578
14. Berriman v Delabole Slate [1985] ICR 546
15. Bettini v Gye (1876) 1 QBD 183
16. Betts v Brintel Helicopters Ltd 1997 IRLR 362 (CA)
17. Beverly Overseas SA v Privredna Bank Zagreb, 28 March 2001 (Swiss federal Supreme Court)
18. Bharti International v Bulk Trading [2002] 37 SCL 434
19. Birch v Paramount Estates (1956) 167
20. Bodil Lindqvist v Kammaraklagaren (2003) (Case C-101/01)
21. Bolton v Mahadeva [1972] 2 All ER 1322
22. British Westinghouse v Under-ground Electric Railways [1912] AC 673
23. Bunge Corporation v Tradax Export [1981] 2 All ER 513
24. Cassell & Co. Ltd v. Broome [1972] AC 1027
25. Cerebrus Softward Ltd v Rowley [2001] IRLR 160 CA
26. Cheesman v Brewer Contracts Ltd [2001] IRLR 144 EAT
27. CIASCO Technologies v. Shrkanth MANU/DE/2809/2005
28. CIDC of Maharashtra v R. M. Mohite 1998(3) Mh.L.J. 223
29. Couchman v Hill [1947] 1 All ER 103
30. Cutter v Powell [1795] EWHC KB J13
31. Dick Bentley Productions v Harold Smith Motors [1965] 2 All ER 65

32. Dr. Sophie Redmond Stichting v Barton [1992] IRLR 366
33. Dunlop Pneumatic Tyre Co v New Garage & Motor Co [1915] AC 79
34. Duncan Web Offset (Maidstone) Ltd v Cooper [1995]
35. Europcar Italia, S.p.A. v. Maiellano Tours, Inc., 156 F.3d 310 (2d Cir. 1998)
36. Evans Ltd v Andrea Merzario Ltd [1976] 1 WLR 1078
37. Federal Commerce Ltd v Molena Appha Inc [1979] 1 All ER 307
38. Fercometal SARL v Mediterranean Shipping Co [1988] 2 All ER
39. Friedrich Santner v Hoechst AG 1999 IRLR 132 (ECJ Case C-229/96)
40. Geetanjali Woolen Private Ltd v M. V X-Press Annapurna and Others (Bombay High Court) (09/08/2005)
41. Ghatge & Patil v Madhusudan, AIR 1977 Bom 299
42. Globe Transport Corporation v Triveni Engineering Works, (1983) 4 SCC 707
43. Gorictree v Jenkinson [1984] IRLR 391
44. Hagen v ICI Chemicals and Polymers Ltd. [2002] IRLR 31
45. Hakam Singh v Gammon India Ltd., AIR 1971 SC 740
46. Harling v Eddy [1951] 2 KB 739
47. Heilbut, Symons & Co v Buckleton [1913] AC 30
48. Hong Kong Fir Shipping Co v Kawasaki Kisen Kaisha [1962] 1 All ER 474
49. Hutton v Warren (1836) 150 ER 517
50. I & G Investment Trust v Raja of Khalikote, AIR 1952 Cal. 508
51. Jayesh H. Pandya vs. Sukanya Holdings Pvt. Ltd. AIR 2003, Bombay 148
52. Jobson v Johnson [1989] 1 All ER 621
53. Katsikas v Konstantinidis [1993] IRLR 179
54. Kenny v South Manchester College [1993] IRLR 265
55. Kihota Hollohon v Zachillhu AIR 1993 SC 412
56. Les Affreteurs Reunis v Leopold Walford [1919] AC 801
57. Litster v Forth Dry Dock and Engineering Co Ltd. [1989] IRLR 161
58. Liverpool City Council v Irwin [1976] 2 All ER 39
59. Lucent Technologies Hindustan Ltd. v. ITO [2003] 92 ITD 366 (Bangalore)
60. Martin v South Bank University [2004] IRLR 74 ECJ
61. Meade v British Fuels [1998] IRLR 706
62. Meeson & Welsby 466
63. Microsoft Corporation v Mr Yogesh Papat & Anr 118 (2205) DLT580
64. Minmetals v Ferco (High Court, England) [1999] 1 ALL ER (Comm) 315
65. Modi Entertainment Network v. W.S.G. Cricket PTE Ltd. AIR 2003 SC 1177
66. Moloji Nar Singh Rao v Shankar Saran, AIR 1962 SC 1737
67. Morris Angel & Son v Hollande [1993] IRLR 169
68. Naziruddian v. P.A Annamalai, AIR 1978 Mad 410
69. Oscar Chess v Williams [1957] 1 All ER 325
70. Oy Liikenne Ab v Liskojarvi (Case 172/99) ECJ 25 January 2001
71. Parsons & Whittemore Overseas Co., Inc. v. Societe Generale de L'Industrie Du Papier (RAKTA). 508 F.2d 969
72. Pearce v Ove Arup Partnership Ltd [2000] ch 403 (CA)
73. Poussard v Spiers (1876) 1 QBD 410
74. PUCL Vs UOI [(1997) 1 SCC 301]
75. Raiffeisen Zentralbank Osterreich AG v Five Star Trading LLC [2001] EWCA Civ 68, [2001] 2 WLR 1344 [2001] 3 ALL ER 257
76. Ralton v Havering College of Further and Higher Education [2001] IRLR 738
77. Rask and Christensen v ISS Kantineservice [1993] IRLR 133
78. RCO Support Services v Unison [2002] IRLR 401 CA
79. Reardon Smith Line v Hansen-Tangen [1976] 3 All ER 570

80. Renusagar Power Co. v. General Electric Co 1994 Supp (1) SCC 644
81. Rookes v. Barnard [1964] AC 1129
82. Routledge v McKay [1954] 1 WLR 615
83. Rygaard v Stro Molle Akustik ASC - 48/94 [1996] IRLR 51 ECJ
84. Sarojani Remaswami v Union of India AIR 1992 SC 2219
85. Schawel v Reade [1913] 2 IR 64
86. Scruttons Ltd v Midland Silicones Ltd [1962] AC 446
87. Snehalkumar v ET Organisation, AIR 1975 Guj 72
88. Solectron Scotland Ltd v Roper [2004] IRLR 4
89. Spijkers v Gebroders Benedik Abbattoir CV [1986] IRLR 2
90. Sunley Turriff Holdings Ltd v Thomson [1995])
91. Suzen and Betts v Brintel and held in ECM (Vehicle Delivery Service) Limited v Cox [1998]
92. Temco Service Industries v Imzilyen [2002] IRLR 204
93. The Hansa Nord [1976] QB 44
94. The Mihalis Angelos [1971] 1 QB 164
95. Transport Corporation v Triveni Engineering Works (1983) 4 SCC 707
96. Tulk v Moxhay (1848) 2 Ph 774
97. U.L Lastochkina v Union of India AIR 1976 AP 103
98. Vasantha R. v. Union of India, 2001 II LLJ 843 (Mad)
99. Wheeler v Patel [1987] IRLR 211
100. Woodar Investment Development v Wimpey Construction [1980] 1 WLR 277
101. Wynnwith Engineering Co. Ltd. v Bennett [2002] IRLR 170
102. Yahoo!Inc. v. Akash Arora &Anr. IPLR 1999 April 196 (Delhi HC)
103. Y.China Rattayya v. Donepudi Venkataramayya, AIR 1959 AP 551

Textbooks

1. Briggs, The Conflict of Laws, Oxford University Press, Clarendon Law Series, Oxford, 2002
2. Arcy, L. Murray, C. Cleave, B: Schmitthoff's Export Trade - The Law and Practice of International Trade, Thomson Sweet & Maxwell
3. August, R. International Business Law: Text, Cases, and Readings, 2nd, Prentice Hall, Inc
4. Beatson, J. Anson's Law of Contract, 28th edition, Oxford University Press, 2002
5. Bradgate, R. Commercial Law, 3rd Edition, Butterworths, 2000
6. Cheshire & North's Private International Law, Butterworths, London, 1987
7. Coonar, D. Law of International Trade in Practice, Blackstone Press Ltd., 1998
8. G.H, Treitel. The Law of Contract, 10th Edition, Sweet & Maxwell, London, 1999
9. John F. Dolan, The Law of Letter of Credit: Commercial and Standby Credits, revised ed. Warren, Gorham & Lamont, 1996
10. Jones, M. Textbook on Torts, 8th edition, Oxford University press, 2002
11. McKendrick, E. Contract Law, 5th edition, Palgrave Macmillan, 2003
12. Mo, John Shijian, International Commercial Law, Butterworths, 2000. 2nd ed
13. Outsourcing to India: The Offshore Advantage, Mark Kobayashi-Hillary, 2nd Edition, Springer
14. Poole, J. Casebook on Contract Law, 6th edition, Oxford University Press, 2003
15. Rose, F. Statues on Commercial and Consumer Law, 11th edition, Oxford University Press, 2002

16. Ross P. Buckley, The 1993 Revision of the Uniform Customs and Practice for Documentary Credits, 28 GW J. Int'l L. & Econ. 265
17. Shearer, I.A., Starkes International Law, London, Butterworth, 1994

Articles

1. A Passage to India – outsourcing: risks and opportunities, Advising Business: Law and Practice, Ad Bus 2.7 (7), 22 Sept 2003, by Shalini Agarwal
2. An Overview on Outsourcing, Advising Law: Law and Practice, Ad Bus 4.3 (9), 9 June 2005, by Dr Linda S Spedding
3. AIR Manual 5th edition, volume 4
4. Confidence and Data Protection, Privacy and Data Protection, PDP 4.8 (2), Sept 2004, by Peter Carey
5. Computer Weekly, 16th June 2005
6. Computer Weekly, 19th September 2006
7. Computer Weekly, 17th Oct 2006
8. Computer Weekly, 5th Dec 2006
9. Crocker, K.J., Masten, S.E., "Pretia Ex Machina? Prices and Process in Long Term Contracts", Journal of Law and Economics, Vol 34 (1991), 69-100
10. Darrel Menthe, Jurisdiction In Cyberspace: A Theory of International Spaces 4 Mich. Telecomm. Tech. L. Rev 69 (1998)
11. Data Protection Compliance for HR Directors, Privacy and Data Protection PDP 5.2 (3), Dec 2004, by Piers Leigh-Pollitt and Osborne Clarke
12. Deccan Chronicle, 8 September 2006
13. Electronic Commerce: An Indian Perspective, International Journal of Law and IT, IJL&IT 2001 9 (133), June 2001, by Farooq Ahmad
14. G. Born, Reflections on Judicial Jurisdiction in International Cases, 17 GA. J. Int & Comp. Law 1, 33 (1987)
15. Handbook of Industrial Organisation, Vol 1, Shmalesnse and Willing Ed, Chapter 4 (1989), 183-255
16. "India" in 2002 Special 301 Report on Global Copyright Protection and Enforcement 128 (App. C), International Intellectual Property Alliance
17. "Indian Information Security", NASSCOM-Evalueserve study, in July 2004
18. India the next IT offshoring locations, Tier 3 cities: Jones Long Laselle (2005,
19. Issues of cost and quality: National Science Foundation, Morgan Stanley Research, Global services sourcing:, Nirupam Bajpai, Rohit Arora and Horpreet Khurana; centre of Globalisation and sustainable development; (CSGD Working Paper No 16, June 2004
20. NASSCOM McKinsey Report (2005)
21. NASSCOM Strategic Review (2006)
22. Negotiating The Schedules in IT and Outsourcing Contracts, IT Law Today, ITLJ 11.10(4), Nov 2003, by Clive Davies
23. Offshore Outsourcing: Key commercial and legal issues, Murali Neelakantan
24. Offshore Outsourcing Means Careful Legal Planning, New York Law Journal, Vol 229-No 46, March 2003, by Richard Raysman and Peter Brown
25. Offshore Outsourcing Part 1: The Brand of India, April 2003, Todd Furniss and Michael Janssen
26. Offshore Outsourcing: Surveying the Legislative Landscape, New York Law Journal, Vol 232-No 52, Sept 2004, by Richard Raysman and Peter Brown

27. Outsourcing – Basic Legal Issues, IT Law Today, ITLJ 12.9 (4), Oct 2004, by Susan Singleton
28. Outsourcing India, IT Law Today, ITLT 10.7 (10), Sept 2002, by Jagvinder Kang
29. Outsourcing and Offshoring: Part 1 The Increasing Globalisation of Information Technology Activity, The CIO Summit, Dec7, 2004 by Richard S. Wyde, Davis Wright Tremaine LLP
30. Outsourcing and Offshoring: Pushing the European Model over the Hill, Rather than off the Cliff, Working paper 05-1, 2005, by Jacob Funk Kirkegaard, Institute of International Economics
31. Outsourcing Work facing New Frontiers, New York Law Journal, 13th Nov 2001, by Joseph I. Rosenbaum
32. Perry, M.K. "Vertical Integration: Determinants and Effects", Handbook of Industrial Organisation, Vol 1, Shmalesnse and Willing Ed, Chapter 4 (1989), 183-255
33. Pre-Empting Protectionism In Services: The Gate and Outsourcing, Journal of International Economic Law, JIEL 2004.7 (765), Dec 2004, by Aaditya Mattoo and Sacha Wunsch-Vincent
34. "Pretia Ex Machina? Prices and Process in Long Term Contracts", Crocker, K.J., Masten, S.E., Journal of Law and Economics, Vol 34 (1991), 69-100
35. Privacy and Security Law Issues in Offshore Outsourcing Transactions, by Margaret. P. Eisenhauer
36. Regulating Outsourcing From Cradle to Grave – The New FSA Guidelines, Compliance Monitor, February 2004, by Brett Hillis and Denton Wilde Sapte
37. Simmons and Simmons International Survey, 2005
38. Successful IT Outsourcing, Springer Verlag (2003), Elizabeth Sparrow
39. Survey of Current & Potential Outsourcing End-Users - The Outsourcing Institute Membership, 1998.
40. The Architecture of the International Intellectual Property System, by Graeme B Dinwoodie, Chicago-Kent Law Review, Vol 77.993, 2000
41. The Changing context of IT contracts, New Law Journal, NLJ 154.7118 (343), 5 March 2004, by Rachel Burnett
42. The Economic Times, 7 June 2006
43. The Legal Director / Wraggle and Co benchmark 2003
44. TUPE or not TUPE? The new pension rights, New Law Journal, NLJ 155.7170 (496), 1 April 2005, by Julie Shuttleworth
45. UNI-Europe: 4th Plenary of the European E-Skills Forum, Gerhard Rohde, Head of IBITS
46. "Vertical Integration: Determinants and Effects", Perry, M.K.

Documents

1. AIR Manual 5th edition, volume 4, declared by Government of India on 1.3.53
2. Allocating Risks in Outsourcing, Arnold and Porter, by George Kimball
3. An Introduction to the legal aspects of offshore outsourcing, Simmons & Simmons, by Jeremy Sivyer
4. An Updated Guide to Establishing a Subsidiary in India, Fenwick & West LLP, by Fred M. Greguras, S.R. Gopalan and Steven S. Levine
5. Characteristics of IT outsourcing contracts, Proceedings of the 36th Hawaii International Conference on System Sciences, 2002, by Benoit Aubert, Jean-Francois Houde, Michel Patry and Suzanne Rivard

6. Changing Landscape: New Legal Considerations in Outsourcing, Global Outsourcing Client Alert, by Baker & McKenzie, Feb 2005
7. Contractual Framework: The Business Process Outsourcing Agreement, Kirkland & Ellis LLP, 2005, by Gregg Kirchhoefer
8. Contracting for International Outsourcing, Outsourcing Journal.com, Oct 2002, by Brad Peterson and Mark Prinsley; Mayer, Brown, Rowe & Maw
9. Data Protection Law in India: A Constitutional Perspective by Praveen Dalal
10. Diamond Cluster 2005, outsourcing study
11. Doing Business in India and Joint Ventures, Varun Sahay
12. EuroIndia2004 Market Background Overview, 2004
13. Governance in IT Outsourcing: Risks and Contract, Deacons Jeff Leong, Poon and Wong, May 2005, by Gilbert Gan
14. Home or Away: Understanding due diligence and contract consideration provides insight for collection agencies asking the offshore outsourcing question, Collector, Jan 2004, by Dennis Black and Gerald L. Jenkins
15. How to Make Other people run your IT Smoothly, by Lisa Sinclair, The Journal, Sept 2003, pg 40
16. In-House or Outsourced? The Future of Corporate Counsel, AsiaLaw, July/August 2005, by George W. Russell
17. India and the Doha work programme, Veena JHA, ed (2006)
18. India at the Crossroads: Privacy & Security Law in India, IAPP Privacy & Data Security Academy & Expo, by Richard M. Rossow
19. International Outsourcing: Some tips and traps from the vendor side, Choate, Hall & Stewart, by Gene T. Barton, Jr., Esq
20. IS Outsourcing – Path to an Agile Enterprise, White Paper, by Wipro Infotech Legal Issues Surrounding Offshore Outsourcing, Masons Technology & services Law Asia Pacific, 5th May 2004, by Peter Bullock
21. IT Contracts Law & Regulations, Infosecurity.be 2005, by Thibault Verbiest
22. IT Procurement and Outsourcing Pitfalls for CIO's: A trial lawyers perspective, Buchanan Ingersoll PC Attorneys, by Francis X Taney
23. Jurisdiction In Cyberspace: A theory of international spaces, Darrel Menthe, 4 Mich. Telecomm. Tech. L. Rev 69 (1998)
24. Key Service Agreement Issues: Service Providers Checklist by Fred M. Greguras and David J. Barry, Fenwick & West LLP
25. Legal Issues in Outsourcing and Offshore Relationships, UNC Festival of Legal Learning, Feb 2005, Hutchison & Mason, by Randall Whitmeyer
26. Legal Structures for Outsourcing, Fenwick & West LLP, 2004, by Fred Greguras, Steven Levine and S.R. Gopalan
27. Metrics for IT Outsourcing service level agreements, Clarity Consulting Inc, 2004, by Ian S. Hayes
28. Offshore Outsourcing & Related Contracting Issues in India, by Sajai Singh, J. Sagar Associates, 1st Sept 2004
29. Offshore Developments: Managing Business Opportunities and Legal Issues, Massachusetts Software and Internet Council, 1st May 2003, by John J. Egan
30. Offshoring: Indian Exodus, Freshfields Bruckhaus Deringer, June 2004
31. Offshore Operations: Industry Feedback, Financial Services Authority, April 2005
32. Offshore Outsourcing of Data Services by Insured Institutions and Associated Consumer Privacy Risks, Federal Deposit Insurance Corporation, June 2004
33. Offshore Outsourcing to India by US and EU companies: Legal and cross-cultural issues that affect data privacy regulation in BPO, by Barbara Crutchfield George and Deborah Roach Gaut 6 U.C. Davis Bus L.J. 13 (2006)

34. Offshoring: Threats and Opportunities, Brookings Trade Forum, May 2005, by Daniel Trefler
35. Opportunity and Risk Analysis regarding Outsourcing Contracts, J. Krebbs, CISA / IG Outsourcing ISACA Switzerland Chapter
36. Outsourcing and Offshoring: The CIO Summit, 7th Dec 2004, by Richard S. Wyde
37. Outsourcing to Canada: Legal & Tax Considerations, Global Outsourcing, Baker & McKenzie, Sept 2005, by Theodore Ling
38. Outsourcing and Employee Compensation, IAM Management Report, Intellectual Asset Management June/July 2005
39. Outsourcing to India: Key Legal and Tax Considerations for US Financial Institutions, Baker& McKenzie, April 2004, by Michael S. Mensik and Brian Hengesbaugh
40. Outsourcing India, Akil Hirani, 844 PLI / Pat275 (2005)
41. Outsourcing and Offshoring: Pushing the European Model Over the Hill, Rather Than Off the Cliff!, Institute for International Economics, Working Paper series number WP 05-1, March 2005, by Jacab Funk Kirkegaard
42. Outsourcing LegalBytes, Baker & McKenzie, July 2005
43. Outsourcing Logistics Functions, Legal Issues in Logistics & Supply Chain Management, Transportation Consumer Protection Council, Inc, 30th Annual Conference, 15th April 2004, by Mickey R. Dragash, Esq
44. Outsource Security: Concerns Growing – outsourcing security survey findings, Booz Allen Hamilton, 21st March 2006
45. Law of business process outsourcing, Pavan Duggal, 2004
46. Presentation on IPR Matters with special reference to the Patents' Ordinance and The Rules, Seminar in the Competition Commission, by Gajanan Wakankar, 28th July 2005
47. Privacy and Security Law issues in Off-shore Outsourcing Transactions, Hunton & Williams, 15th Feb 2005, by Margaret P. Eisenhauer
48. Reflections on Judicial Jurisdiction in International Cases, G. Born, 17 GA. J. Int. & Comp. Law 1, 33 (1987)
49. Selected Legal Issues in International Software Outsourcing, The Licensing Journal, Sept 2002, by Douglas E. Phillips
50. Selected Regulatory Issues in BPO Outsourcing, Insurance Outsourcing Forum, Feb 2004, by Patrick J. Hatfield
51. Statutory Protection for Software Development Workers, Trilegal, Anand Prasad and Biraj Tiwari.
52. Technology Outsourcing: Retaining control in an outsourced environment, by Barbara Melby and Michael Pillion
53. The case for offshore outsourcing in the legal sector, Chatham House, 2004, by Shalini Agrawal and Sakate Khaitan
54. The Logic is Inescapable, Financial Times (London, England) 28th Jan 2004, by Edward Luce and Khozem Merchant
55. The "Outsourcing Offshore" Conundrum: An Intellectual Property Perspective, SME's Division, WIPO, by Donna Ghelfi